Ryland H. Milner

Acknowledgments

The life story of Coach Ryland Milner is more than simply a sports story. Lifelong lessons of coping with triumph and tragedy abound in the life of this well-known coach at Northwest Missouri State University, in Maryville. Success and sorrow are human events that one would expect from a man who has survived events such as the ravages of the Great Depression, World War II, the JFK assassination, first man on the moon and the shattering of Roger Maris' single season record of 61 home runs in our national pastime. The influence this venerable 89-year-old retired coach has had through the years on young people will never be known in its entirety. To be sure, this author simply could not include all the people who share a special Milner anecdote. For those not mentioned in this book, I take full responsibility and heed the words of Coach Milner, who describes his own coaching philosophy this way: "If it's not right, I take the blame."

Special appreciation for their valuable insight and input goes to my two distinguished editors: Dr. Virgil Albertini, longtime English professor at Northwest who also served 17 years as Faculty Athletics Representative and Bob Henry, retired University Public Relations Officer who also served as Sports Information Director at Northwest.

Primary source material for *Dear Coach* involved countless interviews and visits with family, friends, and former players nationwide, particularly in Iowa, Missouri, and Oklahoma. Special thanks also goes to Charles Veatch, vice president, University advancement at Northwest; the Sports Information Department at

Northwest; B.D.Owens Library on the Northwest campus; the *Maryville Daily Forum*; Classen High School Alumni Association and Museum in Oklahoma City, Oklahoma; Jackson High School in Jackson, Missouri; and Rush Printing company in Maryville. My hope is that readers—regardless of age—will find this journey into Coach Ryland Milner's life to be an inspiration. For example, one of Milner's former players, William A. Armstrong, of Lake Saint Louis, Missouri, shares his feelings in a September 29, 1998 letter to his beloved coach:

Dear Coach,

Over the many years we have been privileged to know one another on this earth. I had come out for your football team in 1944, and soon thereafter you told me I could join. I might have been one of maybe thirty or so members, but even so I cherished being able to refer to myself as being on the team. I wrote my family knowing that the family members would brag about me back home. . .I delighted in being in uniform. Overall your having said that I could join meant much more. . .a few words from you meant so very much to me. . .A book would be much more definitive of what you have done over these many years for little guys like me.

To that end, this book belongs to everyone who has shared their lives with Coach Milner as well as those who seek to understand how one man's life continues to influence generations of people. Finally, I thank you Coach Milner for opening up your heart and sharing all your memories. I will always treasure our many visits.

Frederick L. Mares
December 10, 1998

The Ryland Milner Story

by

FREDERICK L. MARES

Printed in the United States of America
Rush Printing Co., Maryville, MO
1st Edition: February 1999

ISBN 0-9670626-0-8

Library of Congress Catalog Card Number: 99-60937

Contents

Chapter One

First Tackle

THE DRIVER WEARING BLACK-FRAMED EYE GLASSES AND A Northwest Missouri State University green and white cap steered his car slowly into the circle drive of the Ryland Milner Complex of athletics and physical education facilities. I am Coach Ryland Milner's passenger on this day. The retired 89-year-old coach and former athletics director at the school carefully parked the car, and then we walked inside one of the buildings in the complex that bears his name. To a person everyone says, "Hi Coach." To a person he grins and says hello. We rode the elevator to the second floor where we soon came upon Dr. Jim Redd, Athletics Director at Northwest who explains to me the story of the daily ritual of the affable Milner:

"He'll come up most every afternoon—weather permitting—some time between one and three o'clock. He'll stop and visit and say hello to the secretaries and people out at the main desk, and then he'll generally either visit with myself or some of the coaches. We'll sit down and visit for fifteen or twenty minutes or so just about the happenings of the day, and then he'll usually walk for anywhere from fifteen to thirty minutes up and down the hall. I know that he enjoys this building complex a lot, and this has been a huge improvement on this campus." Dr. Redd also notes that the office carpet itself is easier on Coach Milner's legs and feet. "He will also go down on the first floor, the main foyer lobby area, and look at a beautiful crystal trophy in the shape of a football there that carries his name and he'll also look at photographs that are in the trophy case, Dr. Redd says. "There's a certain nostalgia when he looks at the Hall of Fame photographs where he knows certainly ninety-five percent of them quite well because of his years here as a player and as a coach," according to Dr. Redd.

However, he acknowledges the daily visits are more for the camaraderie and the friendship as much as anything else. "You knew if Coach Milner didn't chide you or kid you or get after you a little bit that he probably didn't care too much for you," Dr. Redd explains. He adds that Milner checks the names honored on a Ryland H. Milner scholarship plaque "about every day."

On one particular day, I saw that Milner's attention focused on the name of one well-known recipient of the scholarship that bears coach's name. With a smile on his face, he peered from his eyeglasses—he can't see out of his right eye—to the Ryland H. Milner scholarship plaque and recalled a special letter he received from this very special scholar/athlete:

Dear Coach,

I'm writing in regard to your scholarship. I would like to thank you for the honor of having my name associated with you and this award. Hopefully I may have the same success as you, in both life and athletics.

Thank you,
Chris Greisen

This two-time All American quarterback led the 1998 Northwest Bearcat football team to a 15-0 season's record and the national championship of the National

Collegiate Athletics Association Division II. As Coach Ryland Milner glances back down the hallway, I join him on his ritual journey up and down hallways; a journey filled with memories, good and bad from childhood to his high school days to his career as a college football quarterback when he, like Greisen, was a team captain and leader for the Green and White of Northwest. Milner enjoys the memories of his life and enjoys sharing these experiences. He stops and looks at me and says, "People always are nice to me and open doors for me. I try to do the same for them."

Dr. Redd describes Milner as a person who has a "very sincere, caring attitude. He is interested in people doing things the right way. His home is always open to his players and students. Milner and his wife, Luretta (pronounced LuREEta), always made you feel welcome and kind of part of their extended family. Coach was kind of a father figure to a lot of us. He checked on us to see if we were working out and made sure that we were going to class and had our grades up. He just showed a lot of interest in us and made us feel at home in Maryville," says Dr. Redd, who was a football player at Northwest when Milner was athletics director. Dr. Redd points out that Milner garnered respect as an athletics director "primarily because of his knowledge of all sports and his knowledge of people and understanding the psychology of people and motivation of people and being able to communicate almost instantaneously with whomever he was working." Adds Dr. Redd: "Coach Milner has a way of sending you the message pretty strong through some humor."

Robert Gregory, who lives in Maryville and is a former player, longtime friend and coaching colleague, describes Milner this way in a letter:

Dear Coach:

In your 46 years of playing, coaching and athletic administration, your contributions have been highlighted by total integrity, by honesty, and by placing the long term interests of the student-athlete as the top priority. The respect and love of your former players is a dominant theme as they flock to the Northwest campus and to your Maryville home on special days to again visit and pay their respects to their friend and coach and to thank him for his counsel that has ingrained in them guiding principles to lives of honesty, dedication, and hard work.

> *Respectfully yours,*
> *Robert Gregory*
> *Maryville, Missouri*

While Milner and I are looking at the M Club Hall of Fame photographs, Jim Svoboda, offensive coordinator for the Bearcat football team, stopped by to talk about Milner. "I think he's such a big part of Northwest history, Northwest athletics and football history. He's an inspiration to me," Svoboda said. "He comes in and shares it with us occasionally. He 'bleeds green.' He's a Bearcat—maybe the all-time ultimate Bearcat leader."

Success in athletics and success in life began at an early age for Milner. "It was a road that I adopted even back in grade school. I was classed as a leader in a sense. All the kids wanted to do what I was doing," the bespectacled Milner tells me as we look at photographs and trophies. "And I hope some of my old players might enjoy reading the here afters of the old man. They call me the old man. I'm here. I'm going to be here as long as I'm able to do what I want to. I wouldn't change my life compared with anybody's," Milner asserts. "Well, instead of sitting around at home all the time, I like going out to the university and meeting people and talking to kids out there. That's the thing that pushes me more than anything else and those young bucks saying, 'Coach what are you doing out here?'" As Milner talks, he pauses to show me a beautiful Irish crystal football trophy in a walnut display case. The award, named in his honor, has a plaque behind the glittering football containing the names of each year's most valuable Bearcat offensive, defensive and specialty team football players. Another plaque is in appreciation to Don, '64, and Nancy Daniel as well as Kenny, '64, and Mary Peterson for their generous gift of this award, which began in 1996. Also in the display case is a photograph of Ryland Milner.

The life journey of this remarkably young at heart person continues at Northwest. Milner says, "Once a Bearcat always a Bearcat and that's the picture that a lot of people have of me." Who Ryland Milner is and all that he stands for started more than 89 years ago and several hundred miles southwest of Maryville, Missouri, in the Lone Star State of Texas.

Ryland Harp Milner was born on September 24, 1909, in Glen Cove, Texas, Coleman County. His twin brother was born first and his parents, John J. Milner and Drucilla Olivia Milner, already had a name picked out for the twin—Jimmy Brown Milner. "My twin brother was born a few minutes before me," explains Milner. "When I showed up they couldn't think of any name and so Ryland Harp was the name of the old doctor that delivered the twins and that's where Ryland Harp came into the Milner clan in those days."

In fact, Ryland is part of a very large clan that included seven other brothers and one sister: J. Edward, John J., Mancel Pope, Myriam (the only sister), Francis Orvis, Joseph B, his twin Jimmy Brown, and Frank W. "We'd all pick cotton although we were small," says Milner, who is the lone survivor of this branch of the family tree.

Interestingly, the earliest known Milner descendant, according to a genealogical research conducted by Leoneita Casteel Milner, was John Milner, born in 1746, who served as a Captain in the Revolutionary War from South Carolina. Indeed, the moniker of captain one day would once again be placed before a Milner name; only this Captain Milner fought the battles on a football field, a basketball court and a baseball diamond. Moreover, Milner's great grandfather, John Milner, was an ordained minister in 1825 and began his ministry in Jones County, Georgia. That same year he purchased land in what is now Lamar County, Georgia and built Sardis Church in Barnesville and served as its pastor until his death on January 31, 1841. When Sardis Church was remodeled in 1903, the women of the family of Rev. John Milner raised funds to place within it the Milner Memorial Window in his honor. It is said that 60 members of Rev. John Milner's family lived within sound of a beautiful conch shell, which was used as a dinner horn.

Growing up with seven brothers and one sister, Milner remembers his sister in quite an unusual way as he drove me from Northwest back to his Maryville home. "I got a little chair out there on one of my trees at home for the squirrels I put up a corn for. That mother squirrel had gone up to sit in the little chair and a couple of little squirrels coming down on the sides and she was eating the corn and BOOM BOOM, she was slapping them like that (waving his hands back and forth), and I thought my sister (Myriam) had passed away years ago. But that's my sister putting my twin brother and me under the table. She was seven years older than we were. She was responsible—nobody touched us but her—and she would put us under the table 'now you stay there.' We'd start out she'd pop us like that," Milner vividly recalls. "So help me God, I backed up and looked right up at my sister."

Mary Lee Reed, daughter of Milner's lone sister, Myriam, still lives in Oklahoma City and remembers how her mother felt about being the only sister in the Milner clan. "Uncle Ryland has always told me that my Mother—being the only girl—if she squealed their parents kind of lined them all up and whipped them all to be sure they got the right one," Reed says.

In Texas, Milner's father, John J. Milner, had owned a grocery business and served as secretary of the Morris County Fruit and Truck Growers Association. The family operated a cattle ranch and cotton farm. Everyone had chores to do on the farm. However, a poor economy struck the business, and in 1917, the Milner clan moved from Texas to join relatives who had settled in Oklahoma. Milner recalls that the move had to be made so that family members could rebuild their lives and find prosperity. "We just got on the train, all of us, and moved to Oklahoma City and that's where

I guess really things started popping loose," Milner
recalls. He goes on to say his father was a cotton farmer
and cattle rancher. "He was work, work, work. I picked
many many rows of cotton. We always had cattle—
Jersey cows—I had to milk before I'd go to school,"
Milner remembers. As it turned out, Oklahoma City
was where the Milner clan finally put down stakes
because of more employment opportunities. "My aunt
and uncle worked for the railroad. We came in there
and they helped my brothers find work," Milner says.
His father immediately rented some acres out there
and had a cotton field again. For his part, Ryland says
he and his twin brother Jimmy were next to the youngest in the family, and so they began delivering newspapers throughout rural Oklahoma City. The twins
delivered and threw newspapers by horseback. "Of
course, we got in trouble when we broke out windows.
We had a good life, but I mean we had to work hard to
get it. Gosh, we weren't going to starve to death,"
Milner says, "but we didn't have money to throw away
or anything like that."

Milner's mother, Drucilla Olivia is the daughter
of Mancel Pope and Susan F. Baker. Mancel Pope
founded and operated a large nursery including many
varieties of fruits and flowers, and he employed sales-
men to cover a wide territory. He operated the business from 1880 until his death under the name of M.
Pope's Nursery in Morris County and Omaha, both
locations in the state of Texas. Ryland Milner's father,
John Milner, was "a little short guy like my twin
brother and me. . .He would just look at you and that
was enough. If he had to get the switch out, you knew
what was coming," Milner remembers. Ironically, many

years later Ryland Milner, as a father, only needed a similar stare to discipline his own son. Milner says the family rule was "just be honest. Don't go around telling stories that are not true—with a family like ours we all had stories too."

Milner tells me he was brought up in the home to "be courteous—especially be nice to old people and take care of yourself. If you got out of line you got it, you betch'ya and I got a lot of them—I don't know why they'd want to pick on me." Milner adds with a grin: "Yes, I do know. I kid people, sure, I was kind of raised like that. I try to be courteous to everybody." His mother and father—the whole family—were very religious people devoted to the Baptist church, Milner asserts. "My parents they'd read something at night from the Bible when we'd go to bed. My father he was one that we all respected; he never raised his voice unless we got into trouble; he'd straighten us out in a hurry," particularly if any of the nine children talked back to their mother, Drucilla Olivia, Milner recounts.

When I ask him who was the stronger between his mother and father, Milner replies, "most of us would have taken our mother. My mother when she said something she meant it. She was a very religious individual and she was from a big family too. They were very close, my mother and father. I never saw them fight. He was stern about his directions and so was she. I never heard any strong words. I know that my father developed asthma awful bad and he would just walk around coughing all the time," Milner points out. "If we had problems we went to mother and father. If some of us brothers got into a fight, my father would take us out behind the barn and say, 'well who's the best man? Get at it.'

He made us go for a while and bang it's all over," Milner recalls. "He would snap his fingers and point at you like you better not talk out loud."

During one of our conversations at his home, Milner shows me a small, worn Bible his parents gave him in 1926. "I believe in it, and I know there's a hereafter and there's the old boy upstairs looking after us," he remarks pointing one of his index fingers skyward. Although the Bible was the most important book, Milner remembers that his parents wanted him to read other books, too: "I guess I read anything pertaining to sports. I was always interested. The brothers competed on a local baseball team. I was a little squirt compared to them and I always played third base or pitcher. My twin brother Jimmy caught. He always wanted to be up with me in every respect. He just didn't have the ability and quickness. It didn't matter where I was playing he'd be there. We were real close. . .When we were small we'd get on the horses and herd those cattle along. We played baseball together, but he never could make the basketball team or football team. He didn't care enough about football and getting mauled. Me? I had broken bones."

As we talk Milner keeps rubbing his right arm and shoulder. He says he hurt the arm when a ladder recently fell on him. The injury prevents him from writing letters to friends and former players. However, he ignores the discomfort to talk about his twin brother, Jimmy, and growing up in Oklahoma.

George McFarlane, a teammate of Ryland Milner at Classen High School in Oklahoma City, was a friend to Jim Milner and describes Ryland's twin brother as a "happy go lucky guy. He might have been a little bit taller. . .He was just an outgoing guy." However, family members remember a very different side of Jim Milner. Two nieces of Milner, Sue Milner McCourry (daughter of the second oldest John Milner) and Mary Lee Reed (daughter of the lone sister, Myriam) still live in Oklahoma City. They talk about their recollections of uncle Jim. "That's really strange but, you know, all our grown up lives and even through the years we heard very, very little about uncle Jim. I never knew him. Jim was sick, and he died at the age of twenty-seven from tuberculosis in 1937," Mrs. McCourry says. Her cousin, Mary Lee Reed, says she was a young girl when uncle Jim died. During a visit to the Rose Hill Cemetery in Oklahoma City, Mrs. Reed points out a small marker. The words etched on the stone are: Son Jim B. Milner September 24, 1909–January 5, 1937. He is buried next to his parent's grave site. The bigger monument reads: Father John J. Milner July 3, 1859–March 20, 1933. Mother Drucilla Olivia October 4, 1872–May 18, 1959. Reed adds, "the very last I understood that uncle Jim took a job with a carpenter gang or they were digging a ditch or something, but he had TB and that just sealed his doom." Tuberculosis, or TB, is an infectious disease that can affect nearly any body tissue—most particularly the disease centers in the lungs.

Although Jimmy and Ryland were twins, Ryland graduated in the class of 1929 while Jim did not receive his high school diploma until 1931. Family members speculate that Jim's poor health may explain why he didn't graduate the same year as Ryland. Reed acknowledges that Ryland and Jim were not identical twins by any means. "Uncle Jim was, in my vernacular, tall and slim, dark-haired and had straight hair. Uncle Ryland was shorter, pudgier, and blond with curly

hair." Reed also comments that "uncle Ryland and my
mother Myriam looked alike. Mother was short and
round and blonde curly hair just like uncle Ryland. They
looked more like twins than uncle Ryland and uncle
Jim."During those days in Oklahoma City and across
the nation jobs were scarce starting with the 1929 stock
market collapse and continuing through the 1930s. Mrs.
Reed says during that time "believe me those young
men took most any job that they could find. It was the
Great Depression. It was really hard times to the point
that uncle Jim took a job at a time when he never should
have left the house because of his health."

At the outset, Ryland Milner's father felt that his
son did not have time for playing football. Sue Milner
McCourry remembers that uncle Ryland's mother did
not encourage nor discourage her children to participate in athletics. In her own way, she tried to keep all
the family happy and well fed. "Grandmother always—
no matter when you went by there to see her—she always had cookies in the cookie jar and no matter what
time she could bring stuff out of the refrigerator and
put out the most fabulous meal and feed everybody on
a very little bit. She could make something out of nothing," McCourry says. Meanwhile, McCourry mentions
that Ryland "was always my favorite of all the uncles. .
.There is just a special air about him that he always
has such a loving disposition. Always teasing, he still
is a very loving, sincere person. I think he is always
honest in his opinions. I think even though he'd tease
you—and no telling what he'd say to you—that was
okay but whenever he told you he is going to do something why you could bet he was going to do it. He is
always there and able and willing to help you if you

need help. He reaches out to help so many, many, individuals. Such individuals probably would not have gone on to college if it hadn't been for his help and his encouragement."

McCourry sees Milner's daily walk at the Northwest campus in Maryville as a wise, healthy decision. "All the Milner boys have had heart trouble. (Ryland has survived a heart attack and underwent successful bypass surgery in the early 1970s). I think due to the fact that he has tried to maintain good health, and he's continued to exercise by doing his walking every day. I think this is what has kept him going. He lives for that school (Northwest Missouri State University)," McCourry states. "I think his competitive spirit is what has kept him going all these years; He's been out there fighting to keep going." Her cousin Reed agrees: "I think this an inspirational story to show the spirit does live on and go on if you've got the courage to get up and walk forward." McCourry goes on to say, "He has so many friends out there and so many of these people are those who played football under him or had him as a coach in another sport. They continue to come back to see him and he lives for Homecoming. I think that anyone that could live up to his standards would certainly be a wonderful person—would have to be. I hope his life story will be an inspiration to both old athletes and upcoming athletes to show what they can do."

To that end, as far back as elementary school and later junior high school in Oklahoma City, Milner fell in love with the sport of football. The young boy had within him a strong desire to do more than just toss a football around. Milner, more than anything, says he wanted to play sports and one day, perhaps, become a successful head coach. "I always thought that maybe I was capable of guiding youngsters in the right direction. My training at home. I mean we knew right from wrong you know or we got it," Milner explains.

Ryland Milner (third from the left, second row) as he looked in Junior High School in Oklahoma City, Oklahoma, 1923.

A junior high school football field in Oklahoma City thus provided the first backdrop for Milner to show his athletic prowess. He wore some little old pants that his mother made for him. "My sister lived right across the street from this junior high school. My father was over there visiting her. Anyhow, a guy got loose coming down the sideline real fast and I blasted him," Milner recalls. "I hit him right in the middle, and we both went up in the air and when we came down I was on top of him. He was out as a light. My father was standing right there. He jumped out and grabbed me and said, 'I saw you kill that boy!' That was his feelings of athletics. I can remember, through all my years of playing football, that *first tackle* I made in football. From that day on nobody has ever run over me. To me you've got to have the desire to do whatever you're going to take. I don't care what it is. My Mom and Dad, sure they wanted me to play the best I could do. That was all my Dad ever said to me," Milner recounts.

Milner adds, "I'm the only one that took up football. Or course, all my brothers were at the games if they were around town." However, Milner acknowledges that throughout his life participation in sports was more than a pastime. Sports became a way of life particularly in leadership roles. "I played quarterback from the day I first started in football in junior high, and all I wanted to be, more than anything, was successful but I wanted it to come through athletics. Not that I was an authority on it, but I worked on it and studied right down in junior high school, clear on through high school and college," Milner says. Indeed, beginning with high school, Milner garnered respect and achieved success at an early age.

Chapter Two

⸺⊐⊏⸺

Comets

⸺⊐⊏⸺

C OACH MILNER ATTENDED CLASSEN
HIGH SCHOOL IN THE 1926-1927 school year, and it
was at this school in Oklahoma City where he became
an athletic shining star—an apt description since this
school's yearbook is called *Orbit*. Milner gives this account: "When I played I only weighed 135 pounds. I've
been a quarterback every place I ever played. You had
to play the whole game on both sides. I was the one
that kept opponents from going straight in there. I was
a linebacker and then, of course, at certain times I moved
back to safety. If they're going to kick the ball, I needed
to run out and catch it. I'd studied the game. I thought
a little more than the average guy in those days,
whether it was football, or baseball or basketball. Gosh,
when I came home at night from high school I knew
the next morning before I went to school I had to milk
six head of old Jersey cows. What little time we had to
practice the coach expected me there; If I didn't get there
when you're supposed to, I ran laps." He says that Lee
K. Anderson, Ralph Higgins and Wes Fry were his high
school football coaches, while basketball coaches were
Grady Skillern and later Mr. Henry Iba. His baseball
mentors were Lee K. Anderson and later Mr. Iba. The
1927-1928 school year marked what was the basketball coaching debut for Mr. Iba, who eventually became
one of the all-time winningest basketball coaches in

National Collegiate Athletics Association history.

Mr. Iba later coached consecutive NCAA basketball titles with Oklahoma A & M (now known as Oklahoma State) in 1945 and 1946, and later served as coach of the U.S. Olympic basketball teams of 1964, 1968 and 1972. Mr Iba was inducted in 1968 into the national Basketball Hall of Fame in Springfield, Massachusetts, and in 1980 he was inducted in the M Club Hall of Fame at Northwest. According to the *NCAA Basketball Official 1998 Men's College Basketball Records Book*, Coach Iba entered the 1998-1999 basketball season still No. 5 on the all-division career wins category with 767 wins in a coaching career that spanned 41 years (1930-1933, Northwest Missouri State University; 1934, the University of Colorado, and 1935-1970, Oklahoma State University).

All-time records notwithstanding, Mr. Iba was "just a young buck. Ambitious, 'do it , get to it, do it, do it, get here, here,'" recalls Milner who was just five years younger than Mr. Iba. " From that day on I respected him highly. He was the finest coach I ever played for. He was sincere. 'This is what we do, here's what we're going to do and you're going to do it my way. My way and if it's not right I take the blame.' That was his theory," says Milner who told his athletes during his coaching career those same words uttered by Mr. Iba.

A brief history of Classen High School is detailed in records kept by alumni and volunteers of the Classen High School Alumni Association, in Oklahoma City, which claims nearly 4,000 members nationwide. Moreover, Association volunteers operate a museum in the Classen school building which is open every Thursday afternoon where alumni are there to greet visitors. The museum includes Classen memorabilia, such as Classen High School yearbooks, know as *Orbit*; baseball caps, class rings, jewelry, complete files of the *Classen Life* quarterly newsletter, academic and athletic trophies, pep club sweaters, class and personal photographs that tell the story of each year's activities.

Classen began as a junior high school. Land for the new school was acquired in 1920 from Anton H. Classen, one of Oklahoma City's most prominent real estate developers and a respected citizen. Classen was the first president of the Oklahoma City Club (now know as the Chamber of Commerce) and was a leader in establishing what today is known as Oklahoma City University. He died in 1922 at the age of 61.Within a few years, three new junior high schools were built in Oklahoma City. Classen became a senior high school and graduated its first class in 1926.

It was during the 1926-1927 school year that Ryland Milner came from junior high school to Classen High School for his sophomore year where his athletic prowess and leadership qualities began to emerge in several Classen sports. "Usually if you come from junior high, which I did, in football they would (be) waiting for me because I could throw the ball," Milner explains. According to the 1927 *Orbit*, Milner played on the football team, the basketball team and the baseball team. The football team compiled 230 points while holding opponents to just 58 point and finished the season with a record of six wins, two losses, and one tie. In the yearbook, Milner is listed as the quarterback underneath his photograph in which he is wearing a leather helmet and, of course, no face guard. His name also appears in a review of Classen's first loss of the season

when the Comets lost to bitter rival, Capitol Hill High
School Redskins, also in Oklahoma City.

The game was described in the *Orbit* as one of the
outstanding grid battles of the year: "The fray took place
at the Western League ball park, November 5 (1926)
and resulted in a 14 to 7 victory for the Redskins. Capi-
tal Hill scored first on a Classen punt made behind our
own goal line. The ball went almost straight up, and as
it bounded from the ground, Tomilson, Redskin halfback, grabbed it and ran across the goal line. In the
second quarter (another Redskin player) went through
tackle on a fake play and ran thirty yards for Capitol
Hill's second touchdown. During the last period the
Comets carried the ball into scoring distance twice, only
to have their attacks fail, but on the third try a pass
from (Ryland) Milner to Bernard 'Nardy' Cowden resulted in a touchdown for Classen and Bishop kicked
goal. . .the Comets. . .were unable to overcome the
opposition's lead." These two players, Cowden and
Milner, would eventually join other Oklahoma standout
athletes and travel several hundred miles north to the
state teacher's college in Maryville, Missouri.

Cowden and Milner also starred on the basketball
team. According to the 1927 *Orbit*, the basketball team
won all but three games, namely, an 11-point loss to
Shawnee, a three point loss to cross-town rival Central
High School and then a 21 to 19 loss against Shawnee
for the Northern Conference Championship and the
right to represent the ninth district in the Oklahoma
state basketball tournament. Finally, in the baseball
season, the 1927 *Orbit* report states that Coach Anderson had been very fortunate in receiving such promis-
ing material from the junior highs. Among the new re-

cruits listed is Ryland Milner, described as an all-state junior high school baseball player. The Comets high school baseball team made the semifinals of the Oklahoma state baseball tournament and won 11 of 15 games for the season.

During Milner's junior season of 1927-1928, the Comets had mixed results in the three sports he participated. According to the 1928 *Orbit*, the Comets suffered a most disastrous season in their 1927 football campaign. Out of a ten-game schedule, the Comets managed to pound out only a single victory, that being over the Edmond Bulldogs in the season's opening tussle by a 50 to 0 score. The team finished with a record of one win, seven losses and two ties. The yearbook states that Ryland Milner, captain-elect for next year, "although handicapped by size, was considered a deadly tackler and an exceptional broken field runner. His passing was accurate and many substantial gains resulted from his heaves."

In basketball, Coach Henry Iba guided the Comets to the Oklahoma state basketball championship game. In the finals, the team lost to the Tulsa High School Braves by the score of 22 to 17. The Classen basketball team finished with an overall record of 20 wins and three losses, outscoring their opponents 659 to 344. In the baseball season, Milner played third base for Coach Henry Iba whose baseball team won the Stillwater title and then defeated Capitol Hill in three straight games for the 'unofficial' state championship. For his part, Milner started in nine baseball games. He had 28 at bats, nine hits, scored five runs, just one error and had a batting average of .321, fourth best on the squad.

As a senior athlete, the level of excellence rose

once again for Ryland Milner during the 1928-1929 school year. According to the 1929 *Orbit*, Classen's grid machine was confronted with the difficult task of battling—not only their opponents—but low school morale, which was the result of a disastrous football season the previous year. The task of building up this needed morale fell upon the shoulders of a new coach of the Comets, namely, Wesley L. Fry. I asked Milner what kind of coach Fry was and he replies, "he knew what was going on. He was a thorough individual." Fry had graduated from the University of Iowa where he starred on the football field for three years at the signal-calling position. The 1928 season was his first as a coach, and the team finished the season with a record of five wins and four losses. Perhaps, one of the most exciting games was when the Comets faced Shawnee High School played at Western League Park. In previous tilts, two were tied, and, in 1927, Shawnee won a heart-rendering 14-13 battle. The 1928 game was a sensational one according to the *Orbit*: "Captain Ryland Milner, Classen's 145-pound package of dynamite, had broken his left arm in practice and did not start in this game." Milner, who is right-handed, told me about the incident and says that "during practice someone stepped on my left arm and I broke two bones. I was crying all the time but that didn't matter, no," he says.

Back to the *Orbit* account of the game: "When the game seemed lost, Milner was inserted at quarterback and had the necessary fight to start the Comets scoring machine despite his handicap. He snatched Shawnee passes and ran the ends to lead his men to a well-earned 26-6 victory. . .This football season has certainly put Classen to the forefront. Next year she will be represented by a team filled with the desire and backed by the experience to win football games. Only a few of the regulars will be lost by graduation. Capt. Milner, our greatest all-around athlete this year, will be missed not only by the football team, but by all the teams on which he participated. He has been a valuable asset to Classen."

The Comets' basketball team garnered national attention and a place in the annals of Oklahoma basketball history during the 1928-1929 season. Coach Iba led his team to 30 victories and only two losses, an early season one-point loss to rival Central High School, and the other loss in the finals of a National High School Basketball tournament held in Chicago, Illinois. Overall, the Comets scored 902 points and their opponents scored 478. During the state finals, the Classen Comets looked for revenge against Central High School. According to the *Orbit*, "through three quarters Classen trailed; Central enjoyed a seven-point lead in the third quarter. Then Ryland Milner got red behind the ears, and we knew that something was going to happen. Classen gradually drew up to 17-18...Milner was fouled with only a short time to play. Did he miss the gift shot? No, he calmly made it with a wide grin on his red face, while 2,500 ardent fans sat spell bound. Then with only a little while left to play, Classen got the ball with Jack McCracken and Tom Merrick back." Both players would eventually become Bearcats in Maryville. In fact, McCracken would go on to acclaim as one of the greatest A.A.U. players of his time. McCracken flashed his brilliance in the Oklahoma state basketball championship game, according to *Orbit*. "These words came from the lanky center's (Jack McCracken) mouth, 'You go in

Tom (Merrick), I'm going to make this one.' He was standing past the center of the court. He got set, and sent a high arching sphere toward the hoop. Swish! A moment later the game was over. 20-18 Classen."

Not to be satisfied with the state basketball laurels, Ryland Milner and his basketball teammates at Classen traveled to Chicago, Illinois, to compete in a National High School Basketball Tournament. Unbeknown to Milner at the time, he says his twin brother, Jim, "took off, had no money, no nothing, hitchhiking, and he beat us to Chicago." Obviously, he badly wanted to watch his brother play. This trip became a highlight of Jim Milner's life, a life cut short only eight years later in 1937 from the ravages of tuberculosis. Here is an account of the team's tournament progression in Chicago, again according to the 1929 *Orbit*:

"In their first game Monticello, Mississippi, furnished the opposition. The Comets were considerably better, though the Mississippians were very stubborn and the Comets were in danger several times. The game ended 22-20 Classen. After getting over this first hurdle, which is always the hardest, Classen really did run into some heavy opposition, Salt Lake City. It required two extra periods to decide the winner. But the Comets delivered and won 26-23. It was Capt. Andy Beck's smart headwork, and his confidence in Jack McCracken that brought about victory in that game.

"This victory placed them in position to win from Ashland, Kentucky, the previous year's national champion. Ashland was indeed a wonder team. They used some very effective block plays against the opposition. As in previous games Classen was trailing at the half, but Coach Iba had evidently solved Ashland's weakness, for when

Photo provided by Classen High School Alumni Association

Pictured above is the Classen High School 1929 Oklahoma State Basketball Championship Team — Left to Right, Back Row: Wesley Fry, Howard Nicholson, Elmo Wright, Mr. Henry Iba, Shorty McFarlane, Everett Shelton. Middle Row: Clyde Dinger, Tom Merrick, Ryland Milner, Andy Beck, Jack McCracken, Paul Mayo, Carl Sewell. Front Row: Willard McGraw and Charley Dinger.

the boys took the floor again he knew we had another victory in the sack. The Comets play their opponent's game for awhile, then, if they trail, the opponents have to be satisfied with the Comet's style of play. The stalling tactics of Ashland were met by some as equally well-planned by the Comets. McCracken and Beck played great games which brought us through 16-14.

"Warren, Arkansas, tourney dark horse, was eliminated by Classen in a brilliantly played game the next night, 33-22. . .The farmer boys from Joes, Colorado, had reached the semi-finals, and opposed Classen in the same bracket. Although much smaller, the Comets used their skill and headwork to win 29-23.

"This game put us in the finals of the National tournament against Athens, Texas. At the half Classen led

12-11 and was going quite well. However, the game ended 25-21 in favor of Athens. Nevertheless, Classen certainly showed all the teams in the tournament how to play basketball right. Mr. Iba was the best-liked, smartest coach and gentleman of them all at the tournament. Classen has the cleanest bunch of fellows on her basketball team of any in the world. They certainly were the outstanding tournament team, and they, by their gentlemanly manners, clean sportsmanship, hard aggressive playing, won the admiration of even their bitterest opponents. We are indeed proud of our boys for their many victories and the honorable way in which they conducted themselves. They have brought us much fame, and established Classen as one of the best basketball schools in the world." The *Orbit* article also includes information on post-season honors: "We have other things of which we are proud also. . .Ryland Milner, chosen as guard on the All American second team, played sensationally in the tournament. Always covering his man, large or small, they never came too big or dangerous for our fighting little package of dynamite."

Milner still has his 1929 yearbook and often refers to it to rekindle high school memories. He also has carefully kept letters, college yearbooks, photographs, memorabilia and thickset scrapbooks that detail this successful basketball season as well as other sport activities through the years. For example, the following is an April 15, 1929, letter from W.H. Emery, director of athletics, physical education and recreation department for the Oklahoma City Public Schools:

Mr. Ryland Milner
Classen High School
Oklahoma City, Oklahoma

My dear Ryland:
You have brought a wonderful honor to Classen High School by playing in such a manner that you were placed on the second All-American Basketball Team
It is an honor which every boy in America would covet but only very, very few can ever attain.
In behalf of the Physical Education Department, I want to extend to you our sincere and warmest appreciation of this wonderful honor which you have brought to yourself and to the Oklahoma city schools,
Cordially and sincerely yours,
W.H. Emery

Milner capped off a successful high school career as one of Coach Iba's standout baseball players. He played third base, the outfield, and pitched. As the 1929 *Orbit* recounts, "the first fracas with Central (High School in Oklahoma City) fell to Classen 20 to 6. It was featured with wild hitting and quite a number of errors on each side. In the second game the (Central) Cardinals had greatly improved but they could not cope with a determined Comet squad and the final count was 6 to 3. Coach Iba's men did not encounter Capitol Hill (High School) until the finals of the tournament at Norman (Oklahoma) where they beat the Redskins 6 to 4. In a three-game series for the city title Capitol Hill took the first tilt 7 to 6 but the Comets rallied to capture the second and third at 12 to 4 and 7 to 6."

On the final page of the 1929 *Orbit* is a special feature, entitled: "Don't You Think So?" in which students are given titles, such as the Most Handsome, Sweetest, Smallest, etc. "The Best Boy Athlete" was Ryland Milner who won the award over future All-American Jack McCracken who was deemed the "Ladies' Man."

George McFarlane, one of the survivors of the 1928-1929 basketball team that played for a national title in Chicago, still lives in Oklahoma City. During a recent visit to the Classen High School Alumni Association Museum, McFarlane sat down and talked to me about his teammate Ryland Milner and their successful 1928-1929 basketball team. "He was about five foot seven. Ryland was a fighter from all the way down. He didn't think anybody could beat him at anything," McFarlane recalls as he gazes at old team photographs that adorn the walls of the Classen Museum. Although he was five foot 10 inches, McFarlane says he earned the nickname, "Shorty" and played forward on the basketball team. McFarlane explains that Milner was a good athlete because of "his determination. Anything Ryland did was positive that's about the only word I can say. I didn't hear him use any profanity. He was as good of a competitor as they come. He didn't like to lose and didn't very often."

McFarlane also says Coach Iba brought to the 1928-1929 basketball team "a new conception to what everybody had of basketball. He told us 'when you're on offense you've got the ball so the other team can't score.' He said on defense 'never leave your feet; they can't fly over you but they can go around you or under you and they cannot hit another shot over you to beat you. Mr. Iba believed in one hundred-and-ten percent in defense—everything was defense."

On June 15, 1991, survivors of the state basketball championship and national runner-ups held a reunion at the Classen High School Alumni Association museum in Oklahoma City. In an article that appeared in the September, 1991 issue of the quarterly *Classen Life*, Cliff Hansen,'36, wrote a feature story about this reunion:

"Classen athletes who knew and played basketball with Ryland Milner, '29, during the '28-30' era gathered to rekindle memories at the Museum. Those attending were Clyde Dinger, '31, Charles Dinger, '32, Leo Higbie, '28, Russell Fisher, '29, Charles Coley, '28, Jack Gardner,'30, and George "Shorty" McFarlane, '29."

Hansen writes that physical limitations prevented Coach Henry Iba's attendance. "However, via telephone, each reunionist in turn visited with him. Team voices, silenced 62 years, vibrated again—a tearful moment." Hansen writes that the team's basketball expertise coupled with Coach Iba's gifted ability to decipher an opponent's complex game promised a championship exhibition. Here is Hansen's account of the trip to Chicago and the National High School Basketball tournament:

"Coach Iba reserved a Pullman coach. He safeguarded the team's health by taking 20 bottles of OKC (Oklahoma City) drinking water. Upon arrival, the team members were parceled out and housed by the campus fraternities on the University of Chicago campus."

Another highlight that Hansen writes about is a half-time incident during the national finals between Athens High School, in Athens Texas, and Classen High School: "The atmosphere was tense! At half-time the University of Chicago's football coach Alonzo Stagg went onto the court to appeal to the crowd to stop booing the referees who were not calling fouls on the Texas team. With such a knowledgeable crowd, personal fouls could not go unnoticed." In that same issue of *Classen Life*, Milner wrote a letter to the editor: "I wish to thank you for all the work that you have done in making it possible for Lois Simmons McDonald, '30, and me to meet again. (They dated in high school.) It was a great thrill for me to see all of the people I played ball with. You and my niece (Sue Milner McCourry, '54) must be about alike in getting things done. Again, I want to thank you for all the hard work that you did. Ryland Milner,'29."

The editorial directly above Milner's letter to the editor came from Lois Simmons McDonald, '30. She writes: "Certainly many, many thanks are coming your way from Ryland Milner,'29, and myself for the Ryland/ Lois get together in our Museum. Thanks also to Sue Milner McCourry, '54, and Ted McCourry, '45, (Ryland's niece and her spouse) who brought the wonderful party platter and mounds of cookies, all delicious. All those team buddies who came to reminisce were a delight. I think I can speak for the whole group of ten or so of us that we are grateful for your hard work to make it all possible."

She continues, "Now that we are back home we can relive more fully certain memories of each other as we are now and were way back some 60 years ago. I truly believe Ryland's whole life would make an interesting book and, yes, even a movie. Ryland and I enjoyed our times there together, seeing each other again for the first time in over 60 years. He is still the sweetheart I remember of long ago. He remembered things I had forgotten, and vice versa. . .Again, we thank you for giving us the opportunity we will long remember."

George "Shorty" McFarlane witnessed just how close Mr. Iba and Milner became during the course of the 1928-1929 season: "Oh yes. I don't think there's any question Ryland idolized him," McFarlane asserts. "I'm sure that Mr. Iba thought as much of Ryland as Ryland did of Mr. Iba. Ryland told me the last time I saw him that Coach Iba was just a second daddy for him." For his part, Milner looks back on his career and emphasizes "that Coach Iba did more for me than anybody. My whole thought in life was just going to school and try and advance in every day life. I didn't want to be mediocre. I wanted to be the best. All my teammates respected me because I respected them."

In spite of all the success during his high school career, Milner also remembers a very tragic incident that happened during a Classen High School team photo session. "Our big tackle was sitting right next to me. Some guy threw the football like that. (Milner waves his arm to demonstrate the underhand pass.) He said he was throwing it to me and hit that tackle right there (Milner points to his temple.) Poosh, he died right there. The mother of that boy, the whole family, came in and just begged us to play that football game the next day after her son was killed and we did play the football game. We were just dumbfounded; someone was throwing the ball to me and I didn't see it coming. Just throwing (the ball) like this, underhanded but it hit him." Milner acknowledges he felt at first a sense of guilt for not paying more attention to the path of the football. Such guilt over an untimely death would repeat itself throughout Milner's life as a young firefighter, babysitter, husband and father. "I did (have regrets) at that time but I couldn't have gotten to it anyway." Milner graduated from high school on May 29, 1929. He still keeps the diploma in a file drawer: "Classen High School This Certifies that Ryland Harp Milner, has satisfactorily completed the course of study prescribed for the Classen High School."

During the summer of 1929, Oklahoma City University was built and athletics officials at the school "wanted me out there," Milner recounts. "They came to school there and put the pressure on. I was going to get ready to go to Oklahoma City University. I just wanted to get out and so I wouldn't have to pick cotton. I wanted to get a job some place. I knew I wanted to teach school." But for young men like Ryland Milner, the economy at that time forced high school graduates to find jobs first in order to help support their families. So Milner decides to join the Oklahoma City Fire Department making $100 a month: "Why did I want to become a firefighter? Actually it was anything to make a dollar. We were poor people and all of us had to work." Milner also states that the fire department sponsored a baseball team and Milner participated.

One particular fateful fire incident would change his life forever. While on the scene of a fire in downtown Oklahoma City in the summer of 1929, Milner narrowly escaped injury. One early morning he was on duty and a fire broke out. He and others started to go in the building, and an explosion occurred killing two men in front of him. "I took off running home and told my folks I was leaving. I could have been right in that building. I couldn't stand to see those guys perish in flames right in front of me. They were my friends. We were on the same truck."

So Milner decides to quit the fire department and follow his idol and mentor, Mr. Iba, who had accepted a job as basketball coach at Maryville State Teacher's College (now known as Northwest). He was not alone, however. Later on that same fateful morning, Milner ran into Classen High School graduate and teammate, Glenn Marr. "He was working as a typesetter and he said to me 'where are you going?' I said I'm leaving Oklahoma City and I'm going to Maryville," Milner recalls. "I'll catch the next train that comes in here. 'You're not either; you're going to wait. Let me get my duds and I'm going with you.'" At that point, Milner said Marr ran home, found a sack with a couple of shirts and pairs of pants and joined his teammate for a journey north to Maryville, Missouri.

In the end, the reason for the trip north was not only just fear of fires and explosions. Milner sums up why he left Oklahoma in five words: *Coach Iba was up there*. Milner adds, "I don't know just coming back to why we go some place instead of the others. Somebody had to be there that I had confidence and faith in that changed my directions. It was very hard for me to pull up and leave home." Milner points out that his father "just wanted me to be what I wanted to be when I left home."

He and Marr took the train and later hitchhiked to Maryville. "By gosh, when I walked down the way and saw the sign Maryville, Missouri, I kept wondering, there's not any houses around here or anything," Milner recalls. " What am I getting into?" Milner came to Missouri witha nickname dubbed by a baseball teammate at Classen High School—"Taffy"—because his blond, wavy hair looked like candy taffy.

Though "Taffy" Milner left his family in Oklahoma, family members say he did not forget about them. "When he went up to Missouri to go to college and all even though he didn't have much he still sent his mother a little money to help her out," saya Sue Milner McCourry. Ryland's mother lived next door to her, and she and her family took care of her grandmother after Ryland's father died in 1933. McCourry explains that "my mother and father owned the little house that Grandmother lived in. We had a lot of responsibility with her care. But uncle Ryland always sent money to help her out. It might not be very much sometimes but then whatever he had he shared to help take care of her." She explains while Mr. Iba was a major influence, the explosion and fire incident "did have a great impact on uncle Ryland, and he made the decision he wanted to get out of fire fighting. His whole life was athletics and he was so good at it."

Milner's lifelong love of athletics continued in college as he learned how to become a successful teacher and coach like his role model, Henry "Iron Duke" Iba.

Chapter Three

Bearcat Iba Men

I N ORDER TO UNDERSTAND THE ATHLETIC
CLIMATE RYLAND "TAFFY" Milner found when he
arrived at the Maryville Teacher's College in the Fall
of 1929 requires a look back to how athletics were first
organized when the college opened in 1905. The following account is from the 1956 book *BEHIND THE
BIRCHES: A history of Northwest Missouri State College*, written by former English faculty member Mattie
Dykes:

"Physical culture classes were introduced at the
very beginning of the Fifth District Normal School (later
called Northwest Missouri State University) but 'with
no thought of developing acrobats or athletes,' according to the first catalog. The second catalog, July 1907,
announced that the school possessed 'a splendid Athletic Field,' that tennis and basketball grounds were
also provided, and that students were 'urged to take
some part in school athletics'; but added to the announcement was the statement that 'the rougher sports
are discouraged.'"

Dykes writes that the Normal School entered
competitive sports by way of baseball when on July 19,
1906, the Normal team played a town team. She does
not write who won this historical first game, however.
"When Dr. H.K. Taylor assumed the administration of
the Normal School on January 1, 1910, he was inter-

ested in track work as well as games. He let baseball, football, and basketball take care of themselves pretty largely, or at least delegated them to a coach when he could employ one, and turned his attention to track."

Football, Dykes states, at first seemed to be entirely a student-managed sport, and a team was organized for practice when the fall term in 1906 opened. That decision was a year before the Board of Regents approved spending money for grading the new athletic field which then was located north of the present Administration Building on campus. Dykes' research shows that "on October 2, 1908, the State Normal School played, and won, its first football game on the ground of the new athletic field. The game was played with Amity College, College Springs, Iowa."

Meanwhile, basketball practice started during the first winter at the Normal School, but it was not particularly popular with the men until 1911-1912 when Mr. V.I. Moore began coaching. He developed a team that played eighteen games during the 1912 season. In another chapter of her book, Miss Dykes explains in more detail just how "Bearcat" became synonymous with what today is Northwest Missouri State University: Before 1916, the athletic teams of the Fifth District Normal School had no real name. A name was needed, but nobody seemed to think of a good one. By 1915, Coach Walter Hanson had developed some pretty good fighters in his team. In that year, the basketball team had played the Panthers from Drury College (Springfield Missouri) in Maryville, tying the visitors 14-14 at the end of the first half and losing to them in the second half, the final score being 33 for Drury, 28 for the Normals, she writes. On January 20, 1916, Coach

Hanson and his team arrived in Springfield to meet the Panthers on their home court. When Dan Nee, the Drury coach, met Hanson, he said, 'Hello Walter, have you got your fighting bearcats all keyed up for the big game tonight?' Mr. Hanson on his return to Maryville told the story; and the Normal School—now the State College—adopted the appellation 'Bearcats' for its own. By the beginning of the football season that year, the pep squads were yelling, 'Eeeeeeet 'em up Bearcats!'" Dykes writes.

Interestingly, according to Dykes, three years before Ryland "Taffy" Milner became a Bearcat, there was actually a challenge to the school colors as well as the name "Bearcats." Coaches H.Frank ('Shorty') Lawrence and Paul R. ('Pete') Jones urged adding the color black to the white and green and replace the name "Bearcats" with the name "Wildcats," arguing that there is no bearcat animal. Dykes writes that students and alumni who had seen the fighting spirit of the Bearcats told the coaches with no uncertainty that they did not want the school to change to wildcats or any other animal: "Some of the students did some research and came up with the announcement that there really is an animal known as a bearcat. His characteristic, they declared, is that he is hard to capture and harder to hold when captured—a fitting description of college sportsmen on the gridiron or the basketball court."

Equally hard to capture and harder to hold was Ryland "Taffy" Milner who participated during the 1929-1930 athletic season as a freshman at Northwest. Milner majored in physical education and industrial arts. "I knew I wanted to teach school and do carpenter work," Milner says. "During the summers I went back home (to Oklahoma City) and helped my brothers build houses."

According to the 1930 *Tower* yearbook, the administration of the college realized that in order to develop the student mentally, physical qualities must be developed first. For this reason much stress was placed upon the physical education requirements of the college. Entering his fourth year as football coach of the Bearcats was Coach E.A. "Lefty" Davis. The Bearcat football team, headed by Captains Cecil "Twister" Smith and Earl Duse, faced one of its heaviest schedules in 1929. At the beginning of the season, under the coaching of E.A. "Lefty" Davis and with the able assistance of Henry Iba, prospects appeared favorable for a winning aggregation. The Bearcats completed a successful season despite the fact that the team was made of up almost entirely of new material including Classen High School graduates Ryland Milner and Glenn Marr. The football team won three, lost two and tied three. In what was then called the Missouri Intercollegiate Athletic Association (MIAA), Northwest tied for second with Springfield with a conference mark of one win, one loss, and one tie.

One hundred and ninety-five pound football end Glenn Marr is described in the yearbook as "one of the 'headiest' and most aggressive ends on the Bearcat squad this year." For his part, Ryland Milner, a quarterback who weighed 165 pounds, is described in somewhat a prophetic manner: "'Riley' is only a freshman, but watch him next year; he will do big things."

Milner can vividly remember that the first pass he threw as a Bearcat in 1929 went for a touchdown. "'Lefty' put me in the game, and I said 'what do you want me to run?' He said 'you're the quarterback.' 'Lefty' Davis never called one play for me in four years," Milner says emphatically. "I wanted out there, in fact. The players and all showed a little respect." Speaking fondly of Coach Davis, Milner recollects about "the great times we had together. We'd go fishing together. He was quite a go-getter. He was just an old country boy. He was an authority on everything he knew and took things as they fell. Nobody ran over him I'll put it that way."

The 1929-30 basketball season marked the arrival of Coach Henry Iba. The 1930 *Tower* described his Bearcat debut this way: "This is Coach Iba's first year with the college. He completed almost four years of college work at Westminster College (in Fulton, Missouri) where he starred in all the major sports, but took his B.S. degree from this college (Northwest Missouri State Teachers College) in 1927. He assumed the mentorship of the athletic teams at Classen High School, Oklahoma City, soon after receiving his degree. After two years of successful coaching there, he returned to his Alma Mater (in Maryville) as basketball and baseball coach."

Milner asserts that Coach Iba—both in high school and college—"had law and order. He was going to be boss. Oh he'd get excited a little bit." Milner shares one of his favorite stories about Coach Iba. "We were coming back from way down south in Durant, Oklahoma, on a bus in January, 1930. We were driving at night. My teammate Herman Fischer was the driver. I happened to wake up and realized the bus was in Newton, Kansas, and the driver turned left. I said, 'Coach we should of taken the turn right back there' He replied "Shut up, freshman! This driver knows what he's doing. Go back to sleep.' I said, well, we should of turned right back at Newton, Kansas. Coach Iba repeated, 'I said shut up.'" Consequently, Milner says he crawled back in his seat and went to sleep. "You know where we ended up? McPherson, Kansas, just the *opposite* direction," Milner recalls. "When Coach Iba realized the bus went the wrong way, he turned to the players and told us to go inside a nearby restaurant 'and order whatever you can eat.'" Nearly 14 hours later, the bus finally arrived back in Maryville, Missouri. Milner remembers that "Coach Iba stood up and said 'this is a good time for a workout.' So *two o'clock in the morning* we practiced."

Photo provided by Northwest Missouri State University

Pictured above is the undefeated 1929-30 Bearcat Basketball Teamwhich won the MIAA Championship. The team featured three Iba brothers: Henry (middle row, far right), Howard (front row, third from left) and Clarence (middle row, fourth from left); and Ryland Milner (front row, second from right).

The hard work in practice resulted in one of the most successful seasons by a college basketball squad nationwide. According to the *Tower*, "overcoming all of the handicaps brought on by the graduation of many of the mainstays of the 1928-1929 championship team and the inauguration of a new coach, the Bearcats romped through the 1929-1930 basketball season winning all 31 games." The basketball team featured three Iba brothers. Henry Iba, the oldest, was, of course, the head coach. Brother Howard Iba was team captain and played guard, while a third brother, Clarence "Clabber" Iba, also played guard. Add to that the fact that several former Classen High School Oklahoma City, Oklahoma, graduates earned spots on the team, including Ryland Milner, Jack McCracken, and Elmo "Amos" Wright. Howard Iba played for four years, and, as a senior, led the Bearcats through a successful season without a defeat and was placed at guard and captain on the first MIAA all state team.

Nearly 70 years later, Howard Iba lives in St. Joseph, Missouri, some 45 miles south of Maryville. During a visit, Iba tells me about about Ryland Milner. "He came with my brother (Henry Iba). He was kind of a small boy but he had a lot of hustle and lot of work. He just gave me the impression that he'd be a good hard worker and a pretty smart man out there."

Indeed, under a photograph of Ryland Milner in the 1930 *Tower*, Milner is described this way: "This was Ryland's first season with the Bearcats, but he was fast and shifty enough to be of value to the squad." Howard Iba says Milner was a good asset to the basketball team and notes that all of the players on the team "just did everything together. . .one unit you might say a bunch of boys." Iba also explains the coaching style of his older brother, Henry: "While everyone talks about Coach Iba's defensive strategy, his main idea was to take care of that basketball until you had a decent shot because when you had the ball the other team couldn't score." Howard Iba states that his older brother did not yell at the referee. "He might stand and look at him when the referee made a bad call, but I don't believe I ever heard him holler at a referee. He was strict. He wanted you to do things just the way he wanted. I don't think he ever treated a boy badly."

Furthermore, Howard Iba says his older brother wanted "to make a boy think a lot about him—not so much right now—as he maybe does five or 10 years from now. His whole life was basketball and working with youngsters and getting those youngsters so they can go out and battle the world." That and many more reasons explain how Milner learned to become a successful coach. "I'd put Coach Iba first. . .the way the people had faith in him—*everybody*; when you put in six years (both high school and college) with somebody like Mr. Iba you know pretty well every move he makes. I took him hunting. We went fishing together. He was one of the best-liked coaches that ever lived. When you went to meetings, everybody, all the coaches around wanted to see Mr. Iba—just lines of them."

Howard Iba talks about the close friendship that Milner and Henry Iba developed back in Oklahoma City and nurtured in Maryville during the first basketball season of 1929-1930. "Oh, Ryland was always well liked by Henry. Henry thought an awful lot of Ryland just because of his personality and because he was a good player and he cooperated. I know Ryland and Henry were real close. He just took a liking to Ryland when he was down there at Classen High School in Oklahoma City, Oklahoma. Henry just liked his attitude and his abilities."

Tragedy and guilt again entered the life of Ryland Milner during the summer of 1930. Mr. Milner was in Maryville working as a night watchman, among other odd jobs, on campus in Maryville. He was befriended by then college president Uel W. Lamkin and Mrs. Lamkin and often helped babysit their nearly four-year-old son, Dicky. His full name is Clement Dickinson Lamkin. "Mr. Lamkin was one of the greatest individuals I have ever met," Milner states. "Mr. Lamkin was known all over the world. He made speeches all over the world. He and Franklin D. Roosevelt were like that." He crosses two fingers on one hand. Dicky was a little red-haired boy who suffered from hemophilia, an abnormal condition inherited through a parent and characterized by a tendency to bleed immoderately because of improper coagulation of the blood. On one particular weekend Milner was unable to baby sit with Dicky because Milner scheduled a trip out of town. Following are details about what happened next as reported in the Tuesday, July 8, 1930, edition of the *Maryville Daily Forum* newspaper just two months before Dicky's fourth birthday:

"Tragedy stalked into the home of President and Mrs. Uel W. Lamkin on College Avenue last night and claimed the life of their small son, (Dicky). The boy was playing with his toys when he received the injury which resulted in his death. With a small toy in his mouth he fell and the instrument penetrated his soft palate. Treatment to stanch the resultant hemorrhage proved futile and for the second time within four years the parents stood silently by as death claimed another son. The boy who died last night was only a fortnight old when Billy, the Lamkin's first son died in 1926 at the age of 16. This time, as then, tragedy struck swiftly. Few knew that (Dicky) had been seriously injured and students who reported for 7 o'clock classes at the college this morning (Tuesday July 8) were stunned to learn that the child was dead. . .No classes were held at the college today and the flag in front of the Administration Building was flown at half mast."

For his part, Ryland Milner to this day regrets that he was unable to watch Dicky Lamkin because of an out of town trip. "That was the one that hurt me more because I wasn't there to take care of him," Milner says as tears well in his eyes. "Why did I leave? If I had been there, Dicky might have been alive today. But that's back to wishful thinking." (Ironically, in the same July 8 edition of the Maryville newspaper was a sports feature with the headline: "Henry Iba Has Astonishing Success As Bearcat Coach.") As a final tribute to the small red-haired boy, the 1931 *Tower* included the following special page:

In Memoriam
In Loving Memory of
Dicky Lamkin who
died July 7, 1930

The 1930-1931 year marked the fifth year of coaching football for E.A. "Lefty" Davis and marked Coach Henry Iba's second year as basketball mentor as well as baseball head coach. Here is an account of the football season, carried in Northwest's *Tower*:

"A brilliant start, a good mid-season, and a stinging Thanksgiving Day championship defeat roughly sums up the Bearcat 1930 conference football season.

The six additional non-conference games were marked by occasional streaks of good ball intermingled with several defeats."

Milner tells me that he played in the first game on the campus's new football field which today is known as Rickenbrode Stadium. Meanwhile, on the basketball court, the 1930-1931 season again was marked by successful efforts. The Bearcats won 32 of 38 games, including seven victories in eight conference games. Their losses included a conference defeat to Warrensburg as well as two non-conference losses at the hands of Pittsburg Kansas, one to Alva, Oklahoma Teachers, one to Wichita University and the last loss to Ada, Oklahoma, in the National Tournament at Kansas City.

Milner has kept every copy of the Northwest *Tower* since 1930. He proudly shows me his collection of written sentiments from his teammates. Among those who signed his yearbook was Jack McCracken who writes: "Ryland you are a real football player, B.B. (basketball) player and friend. . .and also wish you the best of luck." Another teammate, Tom Merrick writes: "Ryland you are the ideal athlete in my mind the best at S.T.C. (State Teachers College) by far. Please remember me as a pal. I hope we can be together in years to come. I wish you all the luck in the world. A Pal Tom." And listed in the freshman class yearbook feature is a farm girl—and future wife of Ryland Milner—from rural Ravenwood, Missouri, Luretta Gooden. Her photo also appears as a member of Alpha Sigma Alpha sorority. Its chapter roll includes four-year teachers colleges and schools of education in universities.

During the 1931-1932 season at Northwest, the *Tower* staff recognized the efforts of football coach

E.A. "Lefty" Davis and basketball coach Henry Iba: "Both
of these men have made remarkable records in their re-
spective fields of coaching this year." Here is the *Tower*
account of the 1931 football season:

"Coaches Davis and Iba succeeded in putting one
of the greatest football teams in Bearcat history on the
gridiron last fall (of 1931). With their goal line crossed
only once, Maryville had one of the five college teams
of the nation which finished the season untied and undefeated.

"Exhibiting marvelous defensive ability, the
Bearcats swept through the season allowing only Peru
to score a scant six points, and that in the first game.
The coaches built not only a team, but taught such ability to their men that Maryville placed seven men on
the all Conference team." Among those honored was
Bearcat quarterback Ryland Milner who was voted the
all MIAA quarterback in the conference.

The team finished with nine wins, no losses and no
ties. In the only game where an opponent scored, the
Bearcats scored twice on passes by quarterback Ryland
Milner to Ted Hodgkinson and Robert Hodge.

Success followed the basketball team as well during the 1931-1932 season. In summary, the year included finalists in the National A.A.U. (Amateur Athletics Union) tournament and undefeated champions
of the MIAA—24 consecutive victories—two defeats.
The *Tower* claimed the Bearcats were the nation's leading college basketball team and had the greatest coach,
Mr. Iba, and experienced the greatest season in the history of the college. In the MIAA, the Bearcats raced
through the conference season undefeated for the second time in the last three years. In non-conference

games, the Bearcats twice defeated the State Teachers College at Pittsburg, Kansas, ending the Kansas quintet's winning streak at 48. It was payback. The previous year the Pittsburg basketball team had halted the Bearcats' consecutive victory march at 42. After a regular season-ending streak of twenty straight victories, Coach Iba took his men to the National A.A.U. in Kansas City where the Bearcats battled their way to the finals. In the title game, Northwest met the Wichita Henrys, defending national champions, and a team the Bearcats, also known as the *Iba Men*, had earlier in the season had beaten 16 to 14. Before a crowd of 8,000 in Convention Hall, the Bearcats were defeated 15 to 14 on a late field goal. Guard Ryland Milner garnered second team All-MIAA honors and teammate, senior Wilbur Stalcup was also named to the second All-MIAA basketball team. Their careers would cross again when Wilbur Stalcup accepted a job to coach southeast Missouri's Jackson High School Indians. Stalcup then went on to coach at Northwest and later became head basketball coach at the University of Missouri, in Columbia, from 1946 to 1962.

In the 1932 *Tower* owned by Luretta Gooden, of the rural Ravenwood, Missouri area, Glenn Marr, the Oklahoma City athlete who traveled with Milner to Maryville, writes the following message near his photograph: "Toots (her nickname at the school) you're the best little girl in the state of Missouri. You couldn't do better by picking a better boy friend than Taffy." And above the photo of basketball player Ted Hodgkinson, the three-year letterman who is also from Oklahoma, says: "Toots, you are certainly a sweet kid and I sure think you are a smart girl because of picking a curly headed Oklahoman, Ted."

Indeed, Ryland "Taffy" Milner, a college junior and Luretta "Toots" Gooden, a sophomore, were well-known on the campus as a happy and well-liked couple during the 1931-32 school year. In addition, Luretta Gooden is featured as one of the members of the Green and White Peppers, a womens' 30-member pep squad at Northwest. Their battle cry was "Eat 'Em Up, Tear 'Em Up, Give 'Em Hell, Bearcats," and at all games the Peppers were surpassed by none in the spirit exhibited as they cheered the Bearcats on. Luretta also is featured as a member of the Alpha Sigma Alpha Phi Phi chapter of the sorority.

The 1932-1933 season marked the seventh year for Coach Davis as football coach and Coach Iba's third year as coach at Northwest. And for Ryland Milner, it was his senior and last year to excel in collegiate athletics. He did not disappoint, serving as captain and a guard on the basketball squad as well as captain and quarterback on the football team. As stated in the 1933 *Tower*: "In Coaches Iba and Davis, the Bearcats have two men of whom they may be justly proud. These two men have won the love and respect of every man who is fortunate enough to have followed their guidance on the football field. Coach Iba has won widespread fame as a basketball coach. He has come to be known as the coach of champions. Coach Davis is well known for his work in football and track."

"The Bearcats opened the football season by tying the Oklahoma City Goldbugs 0-0 at Oklahoma City. Passes from Milner to Phelps, Jones, Sloan and Hodgkinson were the chief means of gaining yardage. Two weeks and two losses later, the Bearcats bolstered their attack and won their first game of the season by downing the Peru Bobcats by a score of 7-6. The Bearcats' score came from a pass from Milner to Sloan. "Playing their first home game late in the season, the Bearcats smothered Tarkio by a score of 37-6. Milner's accurate passing, Marr's brilliant receptions, and Hodgkinson's ability to snag passes and to run made the game interesting. Although out-weighed, the Bearcats out-fought the Cape Girardeau Indians and won another victory by a score of 21-7. The whole Bearcat machine functioned smoothly throughout the game, and included Milner's fifty-yard touchdown. The 1932 Thanksgiving game with Warrensburg was played at Maryville. Within two minutes after the opening kick-off, Ted Hodgkinson, Bearcat halfback and pass receiver, was injured, handicapping Maryville greatly, but not preventing her winning by a score of 12-0. Ryland Milner, playing in his last game of college football, figured largely in the playing that resulted in the first scoring. Other gains were made by Jones, Stigall, and Sloan. Only twice did the Mules threaten the scoring line."

After the football season, Captain and basketball guard Ryland Milner led the Bearcats to the 1932-1933 MIAA basketball championship. The 1933 *Tower* summarizes the season this way: "This is the fifth consecutive M.I.A.A. basketball championship for the Bearcats, although the title was forfeited four years ago because of the ineligibility of one of the players. The Bearcats won six out of eight conference games this year. The Bearcats played eleven non-conference games. Five of these games resulted in defeat."

Success was again stalked by sorrow, however. On

March 20, Ryland Milner's father, John J. Milner, died in Oklahoma City. He was 73 years old and battled asthma most of his life.

In his senior yearbook, the following quotation is listed under Ryland Milner's senior portrait: "This world that we're livin' in is mighty hard to beat." Elsewhere his girlfriend (who would soon become his wife), Luretta Gooden writes simply: "Hi Kid: Luretta Gooden." Classmate and teammate Glenn Marr notes the following to Milner: "Dear Ryland. I have always depended on you in a pinch and you have always come through. If you just keep up the work that you have started and with the same fight you always show I know you will be one of the many successes that have come from this college." Another note comes from William Yates, business manager of the *Tower* : "Milner, I will hate to see the football and basketball teams lose you since you were one of the main cogs and general. Best Wishes." Another note is written by classmate and teammate Cyrus Slaybauch, of Pattonsburg, Missouri, who wrote to Milner: "Captain. You played good ball all four years. So stay in there and turn out good boys in your coaching career."

The journey to become such a coach took some fateful events. First, Coach Henry Iba decided to leave Northwest for a position at the University of Colorado. At the time, Wilbur "Sparky" Stalcup, who graduated one year ahead of Milner, was the head coach of sports at Jackson High School, Jackson, Missouri. Mr. Iba was leaving so either Stalcup or Milner would replace him in coaching basketball. Stalcup had one year's experience over Milner so if Milner could get the job at Jackson High School Stalcup would be hired at Northwest.

Both E.A. "Lefty" Davis, and Mr. Henry Iba helped Milner towards his goal to coach. As Milner shows me photographs of Mr. Iba and E.A. "Lefty" Davis, he tells the story of how both men helped him land a job. "'Lefty' and Mr. Iba put me in the car and we drove 550 miles east and south of Maryville down to Jackson, Missouri, just to see if they would hire me down there. They thought I was pretty young. Milner says that after he graduated in 1933 from Northwest, "I just wanted to get out and so I wouldn't have to pick cotton. I wanted to get a job some place." To that end, Mr. Iba appealed to Jackson school board members that hiring Milner as coach would not be a mistake. The board agreed.

For the first of what would be a life-long moniker, Ryland Milner was about to be known as *Coach* Milner.

Ryland Milner was a captain
and quarterback of the
Bearcat football team as well
as a captain and guard on the
Bearcat basketball team.

Photos provided by Northwest
Missouri State University

Chapter Four

━━◁▭▷━━

Boys in Jackson

━━◁▭▷━━

J ACKSON IS A COMMUNITY LOCATED IN THE SOUTHEAST CORNER OF Missouri near an area known as the Missouri Bootheel because of its shape. For Coach Ryland Milner, the farming community of about 2,500 might be better described as situated in a heart-warming region in the fall of 1933. Local residents opened their arms to welcome and show respect for their new Jackson High School Indians athletics coach and social science instructor. "My first time down there in Jackson I didn't know anybody. But the second day there, the old druggist had me out for a big dinner," Milner recalls. The new, young coach (24 years old) said his first priority began with preparation: "I would say getting the boys ready to perform more than anything else. If they're not ready, you're not going to win. I had 13 out for football in Jackson." Milner acknowledges that the team had few injuries and fewer discipline problems. "Sure I've had guys mad at me, but I'd say 'boy, get your shower and cool off and come back out' and everything is gone. I never had any trouble." Throughout the Jackson, Missouri, area, the feeling among residents and high school athletes at that time was that Milner was a city-born boy who made good in a country setting. Milner said his first —and last—ordeal in teaching in Jackson occurred early on in a social science class. One particular day he had his back momentarily turned to his students. Milner comments, "It was in this class that it seemed that someone threw a great big piece of chalk that just splattered all over. I said 'whoever threw that chalk up here at me and hit the blackboard better come up and pick it up. And, I repeat, I know who it is and he'd better come up.' This one halfback of mine jumped up and said 'who the hell said so, sonny boy!' Boom, I laid him low. I just knocked him flat on his back. I grabbed him and pulled him up. He said 'Coach don't hit me anymore. Sonny boy, don't hit me anymore.' He took off for 30 minutes," Milner recounts. "After that, I never had a more polite boy in class or anyplace else on the field."

Instead of fights in the classroom, Milner proudly taught his players to heed the fighting words of the school song, entitled "Jackson High." One verse highlights Milner's sports teams: "With our students and our athletes And our Glee Club too, We unite to laud thee ever, Pledge our vows anew." To be sure, Milner pledged to parents and athletes alike he would bring excellence to Jackson High School as soon as possible in his first year, the 1933-1934 school year. He did not disappoint. During the 1933 season, his football squad finished with a record of seven wins one loss and one tie, and in 1934 five wins, two losses and two ties; in 1935 the team finished 10-0-0.

In basketball, the previous coach and Milner's college teammate, Wilbur "Sparky" Stalcup had guided the Jackson Indians to a runner-up finish in the Missouri Class B state tournament division. Milner took the returning players from that team and new players and formed an even stronger team for the 1933-1934 season, but there was a change in the tournament format. Instead of classifications, the top eight teams were chosen at large—regardless of size of school—to play for the state title. Each team could send only eight players to the state tournament. One of the Jackson basketball players was Robert Rogers. Rogers, and his brother Marion, would go on to be standout athletes at Jackson High School and later at Northwest. However, back then, Milner had to skillfully recruit the Rogers brothers and showed just how he cared for his players and their parents.

Following is a July 8, 1998, letter to Coach Milner from Marion Rogers whom Coach Milner says is one of the finest athletes he had coached in his high school and college career:

Dear Coach:

It is very frustrating to sit down and try to put into words the contacts and experience one has had from a person you have known for years. Especially from your coach in high school, college and life after school.

Coach Milner, you were my football coach from 1935-1940. We were undefeated and unscored on in 1935 in Jackson High School. In 1938-1939 at Northwest our teams were undefeated.

I had several football coaches during the war years from 1942-1945. None of these men were as thorough as Coach Milner. Most of the men were from the University of Texas, Louisiana State University and Tennessee. Of course they had assistants and were supposed to be the specialists at their positions. In school, Coach Milner had himself as the coach to produce a winning team.

In his early years from school, Coach Milner taught basic and fundamental football better than any coach I had during my 12 years of participating in the sport.

He came to Jackson High School from college, young, blond curly hair, 145 pounds a young man. He was 23 years old. We considered him one of us. . .My parents thought he was too young for the job as coach. They objected to my brother(Robert) and me from going out for sports. My Dad was very strict and told us it was a waste of time. Coach asked me to try out for the football team. Somehow my father found out about it. That night at the dinner table Mom and Dad proceeded to lecture me, and decided we could not participate in sports. We informed Coach and he said, 'I'll go talk to them.' Coach did just that at Church on the following Sunday and they finally consented to my going out for football, and brother Bob, basketball. It developed into a lifetime friendship.

Coach Milner was a friend to everyone. Besides my Coach, he and his wife Luretta were friends to our family and players. We were always welcome to their home and during Homecoming at college in the fall of the year. His house was the gathering place for players, friends and others to meet there. Always a lunch was waiting for the hungry ones.

It is so easy to close your eyes and see Coach Milner standing in the doorway, waving good-bye to his players.

Sincerely,
Marion Rogers
North Carolina

Back in the days of coaching at Jackson High School, Milner says it seemed like "eighty percent of the players had never previously tried on football uniforms." He elaborates on just how he was able to convince the parents of local brothers, Marion and Bob

Rogers, to allow their sons to play for the Jackson High School Indians:

He notes they were religious people, "hard-shelled Baptists," and farmers. Milner knew he needed the Rogers brothers and he went to talk with their father. "I was a Baptist too. In church one day I just said to him, 'I'd like to see your boys out with me' on the football squad. The father replied, 'No, those boys go to work on the farm. They're not going to waste their time out in football and basketball or stuff like that. They've got farm work to do. They're working on the farm.' I said, 'well now let's think it over,' and next Sunday I was back in church and we got to talking. The father said, 'Well I thought about that. I'll let one of them go but the other's going to help me on the farm.' I told him that 'we don't want to separate those two boys They've been together all their lives and one of them goes this way and the other is going to go this way. Why can't both of them play?' The father reiterated said, 'I'm taking care of them. I said they're going to work on the farm.' I again suggested, let's think it over. Okay. So the next Sunday, I mentioned we've only got eight or nine boys out for football. We sure need them. The school needs them and you'll be proud of them too. The following Sunday church service, the father came up and said, 'Coach I just decided. I'll let them both try to play football too. Get them into shape.'

"That week we had a ball game; gosh, it was muddy by golly, and after the game was over the next day I saw Mr. Rogers and I said 'the boys sure played a good game.' He just said, 'I don't know whether they did or not. They look like a bunch of hogs out wallowing in the mud.' And the next week I got the superintendent to give me a couple of tickets for him and his wife to come to the next football game. They were at the ball game, and it was out of town. The Rogers brothers made one spectacular play after another. I came back and said to the father, 'Well what'd you think?' and he answered, 'Not talking, not talking.' The next football game the Rogers parents were there and when the brothers finished high school and decided to follow me to Maryville, Missouri, for college, their folks came up to Maryville three different times and they drove more than 500 miles to see them play football."

Bob Rogers was a sophomore on the Jackson Indian basketball team that won that first all-class 1934 Missouri state basketball championship held in Columbia, Missouri. The basketball team, the only Jackson team to capture a state title, only lost two games the whole season. What made the victory even sweeter was that tiny Jackson competed with all the larger schools in the Kansas City and St. Louis metropolitan areas and yet came out as the Missouri champion. A similar victory was the stuff that would be made decades later into a screenplay for a movie entitled *Hoosiers,* when a small school in Indiana won the state title over much larger schools.

In an interview at his St. Louis home, Bob Rogers remembers his days in Jackson. He says that during the sports seasons the Great Depression leveled heavy economic blows throughout small rural communities like Jackson. "I think the basketball team helped bring enthusiasm and happiness. It seemed like then everyone was looking for something to cope. It really helped winning that basketball championship."

Rogers points out that while Milner was smaller

than some of the players and only a few years older, the Oklahoman and basketball mentor commanded respect. "Just because he was coach," Rogers explains. "In those days a coach in high school was something. Everybody respected the coach. He gave us fundamentals. We were good ball handlers. We didn't throw the ball away. We wouldn't shoot the basketball until we had a good shot. Coach Milner would say, well run this play and we'd run it. If we came up with a good shot, we took it. You had to play defense." Defense was a priority that Coach Milner instilled in his players as in his own earlier college and high school career when solid defense was ingrained into him by his mentor and idol Coach Henry Iba. Like Iba, coach Milner faced players just a few years younger than he. As Bob Rogers says, "He looked like one of the players. But he didn't have any trouble. I think all of the players thought he was everything. Whatever he said they would do. He was our coach. He told us what to do and we tried to do what he wanted us to do in everything—training—everything. You'd go out to practice and run those plays over and over and over until you could run them blindfolded."

During Jackson High School's 1933-1934 run to the all-class state basketball championship, Rogers remembers in particular the exciting finish against Benton High School of St. Joseph. He recalls in the final minute of the fourth quarter the Indians were behind by three points. Rogers made a field goal to bring the Indians to a one point deficit. Seconds later, Rogers was fouled. Jackson called time out with just four seconds left on the clock. He was on the free throw line and sank a crucial basket to tie the score as the clock ran out. In the overtime, the Indians played a game of keep-a-way and defeated Benton High School by two points.

Rogers feels the influence of Coach Milner went beyond just helping to guide superior athletes. "When I was in high school, I knew I wanted to coach. I majored in physical education at the college in Maryville with minors in social studies and industrial arts. I have always said that Coach Milner was just like a second father to me," Rogers states. "If he hadn't been there, I probably wouldn't have pursued a coaching career. I don't know if I would of ever gone on to school. He looked after us. I could go to him if I had any problems." Bob Rogers did go on to a successful coaching career in St. Louis, and Rogers is quick to point out that the influence of Coach Milner has been lifelong: "I want to thank you Coach Milner for everything that you did for me when I was growing up. I know I looked up to you and if it hadn't been for you I know a lot of things would not have happened. We (Robert and Marion Rogers) made a good decision when we went to Maryville. It was a long way from Jackson and Jackson High School, but we could not have gotten a better coach than Mr. Milner."

The basketball used in the state title game is emblazoned with the names of all eight players who participated in the game and is proudly displayed today inside the Jackson High School trophy case. Marion Nothdurft, who played on the basketball team, shows me the deflated basketball souvenir. Nothdurft, nicknamed "Slim," stands six-foot six. He vividly remembers the days when Coach Milner guided the basketball team to the state title. Nothdurft also was a 175 pound end and a junior when he played on the 1935

Photo provided by Jackson High School
Head Coach Ryland Milner (back row, far left) guided the 1935 Jackson High School football team to an undefeated and unscored upon season.

Jackson High School football team that went undefeated and unscored upon throughout the season. Marion, his brother Milton Nothdurft, Dean Walker, and E.P. Kurre gathered at Jackson High school in the summer of 1998 to reminisce about the much honored 1935 football team and Milner.

"He was the best coach I've ever seen," Marion Nothdurft states, standing near the trophy case. "He just had compassion for everybody. Coach Milner wasn't mean that I know of. He just told it like it was. He just treated everybody like the same as far as I know." His 6-6 frame notwithstanding, Marion Nothdurft said Coach Milner was "just somebody to look up to; that's all I can say." Milton Nothdurft was a 180-pound freshman end on the undefeated Indian football squad. "If you didn't pay attention to him, he wouldn't let you play football. That's all there was to it." He added that in those days, Coach Milner had just a small office space underneath the stairway at Jackson High School. "I bet it wasn't ten square feet."

Milton goes on to say that despite the conditions,

Coach Milner maintained a good sense of humor. He remembers one particular story to prove his point: "The second game I ever played was against Crystal City High School. It had rained and conditions were muddy. I played against a guy across the line, and he worked me over pretty good. After the game, Milner picked up Milton's uniform and told him, 'All the mud's on the rear of your pants.'" I thought Coach Milner was one of the nicest fellas I ever knew. He was one of the best football coaches and he made it simple too."

E.P. Kurre was a 162-pound senior tackle who played mostly as a reserve during that 1935 unbeaten, unscored upon football season. While he didn't get much playing time that year, he acknowledges that Milner had a way of making all his athletes feel important. "Coach Milner included everyone. After a dinner at one of the player's homes, Coach turned to me and said 'do you have anything to say? I said 'well, you had to have some dummies to knock around. I was glad to be one of the dummies pushed around at practice.' Coach Milner laughed like he usually does. When he laughed, he laughed all over. He was that kind of guy." Added Kurre, "If somebody asked me who I would like to be like, Coach Milner would be one of them. He knew what he was doing at his job."

For his part, Dean Walker not only played football for Milner at Jackson High School, but, after graduating from high school, he joined the well-liked coach at Northwest and made the football squad. Walker was a 155 pound junior and co-captain elect of the 1935 Jackson football team. He vividly describes his former coach: "When he told you something—he meant it. He didn't have to repeat it. He more or less had his bluff on you.

He was that type. You usually paid attention to what he said." Walker, who went on to coach high school football in Iowa, says he used a lot of techniques and game plans that he first learned from Coach Milner. "I think he was another Henry Iba," Walker adds, "He coached like him and he thought a lot of Mr. Iba. That was his ambition. . .Coach Milner was always there. He's one of the greatest fellas I ever knew. I don't know of anybody else that I thought as much of as I did him."

Walker and the other former players were honored in December of 1997, when the Jackson High School football team of 1997 went 10-0, the only unblemished record since the 1935 team. The 1935 team scored 311 points and did not allow opponents to score a single point. Seniors on the 1997 football team presented their older counterparts specially designed tee-shirts to honor their past accomplishments.

In 1936, Jackson kept their victory and unscored-upon streaks alive through 16 straight games before losing the last two games of the season as they were hampered by injuries and quality opponents.

Meanwhile in basketball, Coach Milner's team records were: 22-2 in the 1933-34 season; 17-5 in the 1934-35 season; 18-2 in the 1935-36 season and 18-1 in the 1936-37 basketball season. The *Silver Arrow* 1936-37 yearbook notes, "With the winning of the regional basketball tournament, the Jackson High School Indians closed their most successful basketball season in the history of Southeast, Missouri, when they gave to the school seventeen straight victories and no defeats." Milton Nothdurft was a senior and captain of the basketball team which also featured Dean Walker, a senior guard. The yearbook further explains, "March 17

found Jackson at Columbia ready for the state high
school basketball tournament. On March 18, the Indians played their first game, winning from Union Star
by the large score, 44-23. The following night Jackson
was surprised by the strong quintet from Bonne Terre
and was defeated in the last minute of play, 24-23."

The 1936-1937 season was the last year for Milner
to guide his teams to victories in the farming community of Jackson. Today, as he walks up and down the
halls of Northwest's athletics complex, he stops and tells
me, "I think my greatest thrills were when we won the
state championship of Oklahoma in basketball and went
to Chicago or probably me going to be with *my Jackson
boys*. Just a little town you know. But that opened that
front door for me." The path would lead back to Northwest Missouri and the start of a new title: Bearcat Head
Coach. On May 25, 1937, Milner signed his contract
and returned to his alma mater to coach and teach.
Coach Milner was back home to stay.

Chapter Five

⊶□⊷

Bearcat Milner Men

⊶□⊷

Northwest Director of Athletics E.A. "Lefty" Davis wrote a letter to Marion Rogers and his brother Robert "Bob" Rogers of Jackson, Missouri, at the urging of Coach Wilbur Stalcup and Coach Ryland Milner. This is how the letter was written:

Dear Friends;

Stalcup and Milner have been telling me about you. Ryland says you are interested in college and would like to come to Maryville.

I would like very much to have the boys from Jackson with me and I will do anything I can to help them along. That goes for you two. . .so you two talk it over and let me hear from you. Things are looking good for this fall and I want that bunch with me. I feel that I can do as much for you as anyone and I'd rather have Milner men than anyone.

Sincerely,
E.A. Davis

Both the Rogers brothers eventually came to Northwest. Both would graduate and leave behind successful athletic careers in Maryville, and both men have been inducted into the "M" Club Hall of Fame at Northwest. Marion Rogers was inducted in 1983 and Robert Rogers a year later in 1984.

Milner gazes at a photograph of Marion Rogers in the Hall of Fame display and explains to me why Marion "was one of the finest ballplayers I ever had. He was a guard. He could slap you out this way and beat you through there before you get back. On the line he was so quick that the guy started through the line, he could hit him and then go over here and hit another guy before that guy could find out what was going on. The opponents would get a beating. The greatest lineman I ever had. He wasn't a dirty player but he was a mean one. Opponents knew when he was coming."

For his part, Marion's brother, Robert, also has had a memorable career at Northwest. Coach Milner states that Bob Rogers "is a guy that played eight years for me (Jackson High School and as a Bearcat). He came up with me. We didn't believe in losing. He was a great competitor."

"We had an inkling that maybe Coach Milner would come back to Maryville and he did the next year, 1937-1938," Bob Rogers recalls. "I wanted him to be my college coach. Everything just worked out fine."

The 1937-1938 football season for new Bearcat head coach Ryland Milner was a building year. Assisting him with the team that fall was former teammate and friend, Wilbur "Sparky" Stalcup, who later coached the University of Missouri Tigers. The Northwest football team started the season with a 6-6 tie with Peru and later played to a 0-0 tie with Kirksville. Two Bearcat games led to shutouts over Springfield (47-0) and Central (26-0). However, the Bearcat football team did not win road games. They lost to Midland (6-0), Cape Girardeau (12-0), Warrensburg (22-7), Rockhurst (7-0) and Rolla (7-0). The final football team record was two wins, five losses and two ties. Marion Rogers was one of three Bearcat football players selected to the All-MIAA Conference first team.

Milner assisted head coach Stalcup during the 1937-1938 basketball season. The team featured Jackson High School graduate Dean Walker. Also, on the team was fellow graduate Bob Rogers, who was selected to the All-MIAA Conference Second team. The basketball team finished the season with 15 wins and six losses and represented the college at the National Intercollegiate Tournament. In the first game, the Bearcats defeated Sioux Falls, 39 to 27; however, in the second round, the team lost to Murray, Kentucky, by the score of 38-30.

Paced by Co-captain Bill Bernau, leading scorer in the MIAA, the 1938 Bearcat football team completed one of the most victorious seasons in the history of the college. The Bearcats started the season with a 33-0 win against Peru. From that point on, Northwest defeated Midland College (20-7), Nebraska Wesleyan (21-12), Rolla (21-0), Springfield (7-0), Kirksville (26-7), Warrensburg (13-0), Cape Girardeau (15-0), and finished the season with a 65-0 drubbing of Sioux Falls College. Final results: 9 wins, no losses and no ties. Five Maryville men were placed on the first all-conference team.

The 1938-1939 Bearcat basketball squad captained by Bob Rogers, finished third in the MIAA. Despite their four losses, the Bearcats defeated both Springfield and Warrensburg. Warrensburg was on the short end of a 33-29 score on their floor. Springfield lost to Maryville, 36-38. The Springfield game was the last conference game of the season and was played at Northwest.

Bob Rogers stood third in the list of individual

high scorers in the MIAA. Bob made a total of 64 points. Rogers was placed on the all-conference first team.

With the exception of the Oklahoma City Invitational Tournament, and the Kansas City tournament, the Bearcat basketball team won all of their non-conference games. Baker University, the Pittsburg Kansas Teachers, and the Rockhurst Hawks were among those that the Bearcats defeated. The team made it to the semi-finals at the post-regular season National Intercollegiate Tournament in Kansas City. Final record: 14 wins and 7 losses.

With twenty-one lettermen returning in the fall of 1939, the Northwest coaching staff looked forward to another successful year of football. Bernau was once again elected co-captain of the team, sharing the captainship for 1939 with Marion Rogers; Bob Rogers was classed as a first-class guard, and Ivan Schottel, halfback, was expected to add greatly to the offensive power.

The season was opened with a 7 to 0 victory over the strong Tahlequah Teachers of Oklahoma. The powerful Washington University Bears of St. Louis were Northwest's next victim. By the end of the 1939 season, the Bearcats had brought their winning streak in football to 18, scoring 167 points to 20 by their opponents. Coach Milner guided the Bearcats through eighteen consecutive victories since the 1937 season. The Bearcat football team defeated Tahlequah, Oklahoma Teachers 7-0, Washington University (9-7), Sioux Falls College (48-0), Springfield State Teachers College (21-0), Missouri School of Mines (17-0), Chadron Nebraska Teachers (27-0), Cape Girardeau State Teachers College (7-0), Kirksville State Teachers College (19-13) and Warrensburg State Teachers College (12-0).

Pictured above is the undefeated 1938 Bearcat football team with Coach Milner (front row, far right). Pictured below is the undefeated 1939 Bearcat football team with Coach Milner (standing, far left).

Photos provided by Northwest Missouri State University

The team, known as *Milner men*, undefeated in two seasons and with two MIAA championships to their credit, certainly in these pre-World War Two times, attracted national attention.

Co-Captain and senior Marion Rogers was placed on Williamson's Alternate All-American team, named Little All-American in the annual poll conducted by the Associated Press, selected for the position of Little All-American guard by Collier's News Bureau, and was named to the MIAA conference all-star team for three successive years. He was awarded the Howard Leech Medal for outstanding achievements in the athletic and scholastic fields.

The 1939-1940 Bearcat basketball team returned

to glory. Beginning the season with a 52 to 32 victory over the Sioux Falls Braves of Sioux Falls, South Dakota, the Bearcats won twenty-two consecutive contests before meeting their first defeat. During the Christmas Holidays the team was entered in the Rockhurst tournament in Kansas City and was given the honor of being seeded Number One, and they easily moved through all competition to gather in the Championship trophy.

Entering conference play on January 8, 1940, the Bearcats defeated Cape Girardeau 33 to 30 to begin a string of conference victories which ultimately brought the MIAA championship back to Maryville after being absent for eight long years.

The Bearcats then entered the National Intercollegiate Basketball Tournament in Kansas City in March. Victorious in their first two games of the tournament, they met their downfall at the hands of the Delta State Teachers College of Mississippi.

As Coach Milner adjusts his eyeglasses to look at the photos of his 1938 and 1939 football teams on display in the Lamkin Activity Center lobby at Northwest, he smiles as he shares with me a few of the special memories about all the *Milner Men* from both the 1938 and 1939 undefeated teams which were inducted in 1989 into the "M" Club Hall of Fame.

Coach Milner points fondly to two players in particular on the 1939 undefeated football team, Robert Gregory, who would later go on to be a coach at Northwest, and Ivan Schottel, who also would one day become coach of the Bearcat football squad. Both men, who are cousins, maintain utmost respect for Coach Milner, nearly sixty years after they played for him on that undefeated 1939 football team. "Bob Gregory was a very dependable individual," Milner says. "I wouldn't say the best but he was always there. He has been ever since. We always talk about the times we had out here; sure, he was my assistant for a long time. Did a great job. He played for me. After graduation he coached at Maryville High School and they hired him out here at Northwest. He was good help. He was a good teacher; I'll tell you that. He always devoted his abilities on the books. He was very thorough in what he was doing. He wasn't very fast but he could fill holes pretty well." For his part, Gregory says he was a high school senior in 1938 when he met with Milner. He said to me 'you better decide to come here to college' and I said 'no I've already made other arrangements,'" Gregory recalls. In the spring of 1939 he transfered to Northwest. Early on, Gregory says, Milner impressed him and he proudly says the two men have remained close friends.

Gregory says that Coach Milner "encouraged us and helped us in every way to accomplish the things that we wanted to accomplish. He thinks a great deal about everyone that played for him. He has a great respect for Mr. Henry Iba. I never heard him say Henry Iba. He always referred to him as Coach Iba or Mr. Iba." Gregory adds that Milner is like a second father: "I've gone to him with problems through the years and he gives guidance." He explains that Milner has a way about him that you knew that he was the man and you respected him regardless of his age or physical stature. "He doesn't seek the limelight but he's deserving of what he's done in life" Gregory says. "The thing that really keeps him alive is the people who have the respect for him and come back to see him."

Milner next gazes to a photograph of Ivan Schottel

in the "M" Club Hall of Fame display. He is candid about
Schottel saying, "he was a hard man to coach. Well, he
had too many ideas of his own. But he was quite an
athlete. He was a go-getter. He was captain of the ball
club. He had thoughts along that line to call certain
plays. But he was a good one, a good football player
and basketball player in all respects. He was a linebacker. He was a good competitor no question about
it—one of the greatest."

   In an interview with Schottel at his home in St.
Joseph, the former Bearcat athlete, who later played
professional football with the Detroit Lions, remembers
fondly his career as a player and later coach at Northwest. "I knew I wanted to go to college and I knew I
wanted to become a coach—any kind of coach," Schottel
asserts. "Coach Milner was very demanding, and he
was I'd like to say a perfectionist in so far as a coach
was concerned. He didn't leave anything untouched.
Very detailed." In 1998, Schottel underwent open heart
surgery. "I was laying in the hospital bed and I saw a
digital clock that read 2:37 o'clock," Schottel remembers. "Immediately it reminded me of the 2-3-7 play
that we had when I played for Coach Milner; that meant
the two back got the ball, three-back came around and
went around the seven hole. That was my favorite play.
That's the play I scored my first touchdown. I could
draw the play. Now that's been almost 60 years ago. I
was taught pretty good to remember that play."

   When I tell Schottel that Milner describes him as a
hard football player to coach, Schottel responds: "I guess
you could maybe say that. Starting two consecutive
undefeated football seasons (1938-1939) I just felt like
we were supposed to win when we went out on the field.

I think we took each game as it came." Schottel vividly remembers another Milner moment: "Before the game with Washington University in St. Louis we were scheduled to have a short workout, pack and leave for St. Louis. I left school and went home to grab a little nap. Somehow or another, my alarm didn't go off and I woke up and I thought, 'Oh my God' and I ran to the field. I thought maybe Coach Milner and the team had already left. But it just so happened that they were out on the field. So, I ran down, dressed in my football uniform right quick and came out on the field. Coach Milner looked at me—and I never will forget it—he said, *'well, if it isn't old Rip Van Winkle.* Well, get on the track and start running.' Coach Milner knew how to handle me or I would've been gone long ago."

Schottel describes Milner as a fierce competitor. "We could come in at the half leading by twenty or twenty-five points and he'd just hit the roof like we hadn't begun to play yet," Schottel recounts. "Every game was important. We worked hard. Coach Milner could see more things happen in a football play during a game than any person I ever saw. If I made one mistake in the game, Coach Milner was sure going to see it." Schottel illustrates Milner's observant eyes with the following story. Schottel says he was late for Milner's retirement banquet held in Maryville, so he sat over on the floor against a wall. Finally, Coach Milner got up to say a few words. Schottel recalls Milner's words: "There's a guy sitting over against the wall here. Ivan Schottel was the finest blocking back I ever saw in any stadium."

Milner has high principles and "he won't come off of them—not one iota. He's been a great coach and a great leader," Schottel explains. Another special moment came when Milner visited Schottel in a hospital in St. Joseph, Missouri. "He'd had been through this kind of heart surgery and he told me, 'don't be afraid. It's not that bad,' Schottel recalls. "There was no fear. I wasn't afraid at all. I can't tell you word for word what I mean when I say there's something special between Coach Milner and me—it's been going on for 60 years. How many times he's gone to bat for me and how many times I've laid it on the line for him," Schottel reflects as his voice trails off.

Ryland Milner's football teams from 1940 until 1943 experienced both victories and few losses. In 1940 the Bearcat football team was 7-2-0, the 1941 team 6-2-1, the 1942 team 4-2-1, and the 1943 team with a record of 5-1-1.

In the 1944 football season, however, a new winning streak was started. Only his fighting soldiers for the most part were Navy personnel who came to Northwest during the war years.

Chapter Six

━━◖◯◗━━

V-12ers

━━◖◯◗━━

COACH RYLAND MILNER'S 1944 BEARCAT FOOTBALL TEAM AT NORTHWEST CAN can lay claim to an accomplishment that only the 1931, 1938, and 1939 teams as well as the 1998 Bearcat football national champions can match. The players on the gridiron finished the 1944 season undefeated and untied with a a 7-0 record and was one of only ten teams in the nation to go undefeated. The team received special recognition by being invited to the Sun Bowl. No Northwest grid squad, before or since, has ever received a bowl bid. However, the invitation had to be turned down. Why? These were not just football players. They were predominantly United States Navy trainees who had to leave after the regular season for other military assignments. They were members of the United States Navy V-12 unit. Coach Milner describes the Naval trainees as "the greatest bunch of kids that I ever had anything to do with. Not that they were better than anybody else, necessarily, but they were all young individuals—no two from the same town—always different and they were just ready all of the time." Coach Milner explains that several hundred Naval trainees came to Northwest as part of President Franklin D. Roosevelt's program known as the V-12 to provide officer candidates an education and prepare these young men both mentally and physically to better serve as naval officers for the United States.

The 1944 V-12 Undefeated Football Team. . .

"Maybe in some cases it was a way to get the young kids off the streets, get them into a program. They weren't old enough to be drafted. They just assigned them to a certain college," Milner asserts. Assisting Milner on the coaching staff were Bob Dorrah, from Victorville, Illinois, and Dr. John Harr, former professor and chair of the history department.

Milner says the V-12 program came to campus primarily because of Northwest President Uel Lamkin's friendship with President Franklin D. Roosevelt. "We were way out in the country compared to the big cities where they were going to sign kids off the streets and come in," Milner recalls. "We didn't have to my knowl-

. .Inducted in 1994 into M Club Hall of Fame

Photo provided by Northwest Missouri State University

edge mean kids in the V-12 program at all. If they were, they got straightened out in a hurry."

The 1944 V-12 undefeated football team was inducted in 1994 into the "M" Club Hall of Fame at Northwest. The roster includes a few non-military personnel from Maryville. Following is the team roster of the players on Milner's third undefeated football team at Northwest :

William Faust, Chicago, Illinois; Don Barber, Skidmore, Missouri; Blaine Steck, Tarkio, Missouri; Lloyd Hunke, Enid, Oklahoma; Raymon McIlroy, Lamesa, Texas; John Fisher, Souderton, Pennsylvania; Orville Buchanan, Louisiana, Missouri; John Brown,

Hartley, Texas; Ted Sharp, St. Joseph, Missouri; Jim Corken, Maryville, Missouri; Emil Matyas, Uniontown, Pennsylvania; Joe DeBonis, Wilkes-Barre, Pennsylvania; Ned Bishop, Monett, Missouri; George Campbell, Ottawa, Kansas; Louis Vieceli, Johnston City, Illinois; James Swanson, Lincoln, Nebraska; John Williams, Independence, Missouri; Bob Shillito, Overland, Missouri; Julius Stagner, Van, Texas; Norman Penfold, Kansas City, Missouri; Basil Smith, El Paso, Texas; M.B. Huntley, Elmira, New York; Jerome Zukauskas, Chicago, Illinois; Paul Petrofsky, Henderson, Texas; Bill Hooper, Maryville, Missouri; William Armstrong, St. Louis, Missouri; Eugene Becker, Erie, Pennsylvania; William Schneidau, Buffalo, New York; Charles Curington, Boerne, Texas; Bob Grubbs, St. Louis, Missouri; Jack Holmes, Holliday, Texas; Jim Allen, El Campo, Texas; Archie Allen, Sedalia, Missouri; Bill Aitken, Normandy, Missouri; Dick Stempel, Doylestown, Pennsyvlvania; Irving Rose, Texarkana, Texas; Jack Dieterich, Maryville, Missouri; Richard Crump, Mexico; Morris Galter, Lincoln, Nebraska; George Watson, St. Joseph, Missouri; Glenn Sullivan, St. Joseph, Missouri; Maurice McClish, Amarillo, Texas; Don Hickok, Ulysses, Kansas; Leonard Marchinski, Mt. Carmel, Pennsylvania; Joe Smith, Brooklyn, New York; Glen Grant, Sikeston, Missouri; Austin Embree, Andrews, Texas; Kenneth Johann, Evansville, Indiana; Joe Dorough, Denver, Colorado; Bob Hutchinson, St. Joseph, Missouri; Bob Ambrose, Maryville, Missouri; Ben Hearne, Amarillo, Texas; John Herron, hometown not listed, and Arthur Walsh, Chicago, Illinois.

Robert Dorrah now lives in Sedalia, Missouri. During a visit to his home, Dorrah talks about the V-12 unit and working for Ryland Milner.

"I went into the Navy in 1943 and I was stationed at Maryville. I just got out of high school two years before and I had played football in Illinois," Dorrah recalls. "Coach Milner asked me, 'Could you be my line coach?' and I said, 'if you want me to be line coach, I'll be a line coach.'" Dorrah remembers he lived right in the residence halls at Northwest with the V-12 football team. The football players would practice fifteen minutes a day and some days try to get in at least an hour of football drills. Dorrah explains that the V-12 football players "always were in a hurry. They ran all the time. We didn't have a couple of big fellas because you were limited in the V-12 program for weight because they had to meet certain standards to get in. They were fast."

Dorrah describes Milner as "straightforward. If you were a friend of Ryland's you were a friend always with him. We stayed together bird hunting all the time. We would go out and we'd be walking alone he'd say, 'now here's what I want this end to do or this tackle to do, or the guard to do and the center.'" Dorrah adds, "You had to take his words and put them into action."

One memorable event illustrates how Milner's words turned into action. Dorrah was driving the team bus on the way to a scheduled game in Pittsburg, Kansas. "I was driving down the hill going into Pittsburg; we had four or five miles to go when something went off and it banged. Coach Milner said, 'What's that? What's that?'" I said, 'we have a flat tire.' I let the bus coast down to the bottom of the hill. When we got down there, we went to get the jack out to put the new tire in." To the surprise of Dorrah, there was no jack on the bus. "So Coach Milner called for all of the biggest boys. He put them here, there and all around the bus and he said to his players, 'Okay we're going to pick the bus up.' So we picked up the bus and held it up and they took the flat tire off and put on the new tire. Coach Milner then told his players 'All right, load up load up.' We were running a little late.' Coach Milner never said another word to them about picking up that bus."

Dorrah states that Milner was a coach who was always a play or two ahead of the game. "If you get in a group with him, you're not a stranger. He's helped me continue what I believe about being honest and truthful."

Fifty years after the 1944 team went undefeated, a reunion of V-12 personnel was held in 1994 on the Northwest campus. Surviving V-12ers presented Coach Milner with a special plaque when the team was inducted into the "M" Club Hall of Fame. The plaque read: "In recognition of your dedication and commitment to Northwest Missouri State University and the U.S. Navy V-12 Personnel of World War Two. You made men from boys, instilling a competitive spirit, integrity and values. Building character that has met the test of time in a competitive world. With gratitude from your undefeated football team of 1944 Hall of Fame October 14, 1994."

In addition, the V-12 unit presented Milner with a unique two-foot trophy. During the reunion in Maryville, they convinced their old coach to attend the local movie theater where the movie was "Grumpy Old Men." "That Navy group came and got me and took me and said you're going to go. So I went with them," Coach Milner reflects. "Just before the show was over, they said nobody leave; they had something to do. They called me up there and presented me a trophy with the words 'Grumpy Old Man' because I had a V-12 program, and they said I was so grumpy they couldn't get along with me." Coach Milner says the humorous award was "great. If they thought enough of me to call me a grumpy old man, I love them. I love them all."

Players from that V-12 football team have expressed their appreciation to their coach, Ryland Milner, through special letters. Following is a letter written in 1998 by Ned Bishop, a member of the 1944 undefeated team:

Dear Coach;

I think of you often as I go through my daily activities.

I lost my father when I was three and you became my father figure when I came to Northwest Missouri State Teachers College in 1943. The commitment, discipline, effort and execution you demanded, and the principles you espoused provided the foundation that allowed me to endure and overcome the many obstacles that each of us must face as we enter the real world. Through W.W.II, marriage, raising a family and a working career, the lessons you taught guided me and gave me the tools to manage each phase of my life.

Margie, my wife of 52 years, and a Maryville girl who has known you longer than I, said 'you were,' and some say still are, 'a tough and gruff guy with a huge Teddy Bear heart.' Your soft and caring heart has helped so many of your students to attend and finish school, that the impact on society will ever be known.

As I look back, life has been good to me and my

family and I owe much of it to you and your tough and loving care.

> *Ned Bishop*
> *V-12 unit.*
> *Scottsdale, Arizona*

The impact Coach Milner has had on other V-12 unit servicemen is exemplified in an insightful letter from an injured football player who watched the games mostly from the sidelines:

Dear Coach:

I think back to the mid-1940s and your name comes to mind. To me you were among the finest gentlemen the Navy could have selected to mold young people!! I remember I was injured in practice by a crack-back block on my right knee. It put me out of commission for most of the season but never out of touch with the progress of the team. Coach, you taught us that all our plans didn't always mature, but we kept on trying. I will never forget your sincerity, hard drive, kindness, and understanding. You made some good men out of the people in the V-12 unit.

> *My very best to you Coach,*
> *Raymon McIlroy*
> *V-12 unit*
> *Lubbock, Texas*

Perhaps no letter puts into perspective the influence Coach Milner had on the V-12ers than the words penned by George Campbell. In 1994, the same year that the 1944 team was inducted into the "M" Club Hall of Fame, Campbell was inducted for his individual football achievements. Following is Campbell's letter to Ryland Milner:

June 6, 1998

Dear Coach:

It has been fifty-four years since the Allies made their D-Day landings on the beaches of Normandy, France, and I was stationed in the U.S. Navy V-12 unit at Maryville, Missouri. But in many ways it seems like it was only yesterday that I was a student at Northwest Missouri State University.

I had enlisted in the U.S. Navy V-5 program (naval aviation cadet) when I was seventeen years old. I had expected to be flying U.S. Navy airplanes in the Pacific Ocean area, where my older brother was.

However, we were told there would be a slight delay while we finished a semester or so of college in a V-12 Unit. It turned out to be three semesters at Northwest Missouri State.

During the time we were in college we were allowed to participate in all campus activities. I got to play football for you at Northwest Missouri State..

I can truly say I enjoyed every minute of it although I felt at the time that I should have been in combat. Later I was in combat in Korea.

We had many good leaders and professors but I always felt you were one of the best. In all the years since I left Northwest Missouri State, I have looked back with fond memories of you and the college.

In 1947 I coached the Eighth Marines football team and there I fully realized what a good coach you had been to us. As I have told all of my friends many times, you are an exceptional man.

Besides having a great record you had the unusual ability to take a neophyte team like our 1944 team and mold it into a winning one. I believe that ability is the mark of an outstanding coach in any conference.

One of my favorite poems, 'A Psalm of Life' by Henry Wadsworth Longfellow, states:

> *'Lives of great men all remind us*
> *We can make our lives sublime*
> *And, departing, leave behind us*
> *Footprints on the sands of time.'*

From the 1920s through the 1990s as a student athlete, coach, director of athletics and friend you have certainly left your footprints on Northwest's sands of time.

I have always thought that the naming of their buildings and facilities at Northwest for their outstanding faculty members and administrators was an excellent idea. Therefore, it seemed highly appropriate that the sports complex was designated as the Ryland Milner Complex in your honor since you truly deserved the honor.

You have been an inspiration to the student athletes and friends of Northwest Missouri State, and rate a salute with a commendation for a job 'well done.'

> *Sincerely.*
> *George Willis Campbell*
> *1944 Football Team*
> *U.S. Navy V-12*
> *Topeka, Kansas*

I pored through all the many cards and letters from V-12 survivors and read each one to Milner. The venerable coach rekindled memories about the author of each letter or card. To be sure, it became quite clear that all the correspondence went beyond just respect for a coach. Rather, it is the mutual love and admiration for a man who became a father figure and lifelong friend. Milner admits he is frustrated that a shoulder injury and poor eyesight prevents him from writing letters to his many friends nationwide. "I want everyone to know that I think about them all the time. It's so nice that these players remember me," he poignantly remarks as we walk outside of his Maryville home to check his mailbox. He received two more letters from former players. "I think about them all the time and I wish them all the best." Milner also remembers daily his beloved wife, Luretta, and their first son. Once again, Milner would face more tragedy and triumph.

Luretta Milner
November 1, 1912 - March 9, 1980

Chapter Seven

Luretta and Jimmie

WHEN LURETTA GOODEN OF RURAL RAVENWOOD, MISSOURI, graduated from Northwest with a degree in home economics, next to her senior portrait in the 1934 *Tower* is the following statement: "She's the girl who won the man who won the championship." That man was Ryland Harp Milner who had graduated the year earlier in the spring of 1933. The couple married the day after Christmas of 1934 at the Nodaway County Courthouse in Maryville. "Who was my biggest fan in the entire world?" Coach Milner poses to me. "My wife Luretta. She'd get over in the corner and sit and watch the ball games. She was a good basketball player in high school herself over at Ravenwood."

Coach Milner said that Luretta was "one of the better-liked women in Maryville. She was just a local gal who would do anything in the world for you. In ball games she was a cheerleader and everything else. I loved her until the day they put her in the grave in 1980; I will always love Luretta." She died from emphysema at age 67. Milner adds, "Our marriage was better than any athletic records on the sports fields. She was there all the time. I doubt if I would have been successful without Luretta in my life." In fact, the "M" Club Hall of Fame display located on the Northwest campus includes a plaque with the words "NWMSU-

Athletic Hall of Fame Donated by Friends of Luretta
Milner. Luretta E. (Ethel) Milner November 1, 1912 –
March 9, 1980. Her portrait is located right in the
middle of the glass display case for visitors to see all
the individuals inducted into the school's Hall of Fame.
As Milner peers from his eyeglasses toward the portrait of his best friend and lifelong partner, he says,
"She was a beautiful lady. . . Oh you thank the Lord
you still remember her. Light blue eyes, brown hair,"
as his voice trails off. After a short pause, Milner adds,
"I expect it was love at first sight. I have all kinds of
photographs of her. Beautiful gal. We met in college in
1931-1932. Who had a nickel or dime to go the picture
show? Everybody loved Luretta. She had no enemies.
She liked anything I participated in. She was just an
old country gal over there on a big farm."

Sue Milner McCourry, Milner's niece and a resident of Oklahoma City, fondly remembers aunt Luretta.
"She was a wonderful person. She was petite and she
was an immaculate housekeeper. You could eat off her
floors. They were sparkling clean, and she moved the
furniture and ran the sweeper every day and dusted
everything from top to bottom. She just had all kinds of
energy," McCourry says. "I think they were a really neat
couple. They had a very good open relationship with
one another, a very good line of communication and they
enjoyed entertaining together. Aunt Luretta lived
every moment of these football and basketball players.
Their house was full of athletes all the time. Uncle
Ryland had a lot of dignity and respect for her. When
aunt Luretta died in 1980, it was terrible and it was
devastating to him. He really was not ready at that age
to give her up. She had a hard struggle and it was an

unfortunate thing. He could have given up but he didn't. He picked up the pieces and went on. It was the school (Northwest). I think if it hadn't been for the school he wouldn't have lasted."

For her part, Mary Lee Reed, another niece of Ryland Milner who also lives in Oklahoma City, recalls that "Luretta understood him right to the minute detail. Oh, she knew him and loved him and tolerated his ornery behavior."

Maryville resident Ken B. Jones, retired commissioner of the then Missouri Intercollegiate Athletic Association (now named the Mid-America Intercollegiate Athletics Association) and a former player for Milner, remembers the couple this way: "Luretta was a laid back lady, a class person. In terms of their relationship, they were very close. That was just as an outside observer. I think he listened to her, and I think she influenced him in her quiet way." When Luretta died, Jones adds, his dear friend Milner was more than just devastated. "I don't know that he's ever recovered fully. I mean no one might. I know that it was just quite a blow for him."

Bill Coulter, of Lexington, Missouri, and a former player under Milner, remembers how so in love the Milners were. "One of the things that I remember always was when we (college team) stopped to eat on the way home from a ball game, he bought Luretta a box of candy to take home. Everybody talks about they loved Ryland Milner, but the reason they did is because Ryland Milner loved them. I don't know that any of us will ever be able to describe the impact that Coach Milner and Luretta had for our own lives. Talk about words like integrity, competitiveness—they had it all for us."

Coulter goes on to say, "I think probably one of things I remember about Coach Milner is that he took care of his athletes. I was hurt one year and found out that I could get some medication that would let me play on a leg that was hurt. The thing that will stay with me a long time is when Coach Milner said to me, 'Billy you have a heck of a lot longer to walk on that leg than you do to play on it.' I wanted to play and I didn't care what kind of medication I was taking. I was not going to play a down for Coach Milner until he was satisfied that the injury was healed."

Coulter further emphasizes,"I personally think that if Ryland Milner is not a genius so far as football tactics were concerned he is near genius. He is inventive, he has a great imagination, and I think all his players carried that away with them. Mr. Iba kind of rubbed off on us through Coach Milner who said when we went out to coach 'don't you worry about popularity. You worry about respect and if you have the respect of a high school kid during his high school years, you'll be popular with him when the time comes that it's important.' Coach Milner gave of himself and that's why we all love him so. He always has time for us, and young people today need to know that's the way it works."

To be sure, Ivan Schottel said Ryland and Luretta "were the greatest. Luretta just lived and died with the Bearcats. They were just like family and they were concerned with you. If you did something wrong, Luretta would chew you out just as well as Coach Milner." For Coulter, Schottel, Jones and many other former athletes of Ryland Milner, one tragic accident brought an outpouring love and widespread support to Ryland and Luretta Milner.

The same school year of the undefeated V-12 football team, 1944, was also the year that Ryland and Luretta Milner became the proud parents of their first child, a son James "Jimmie" Ryland Milner. Their son was born on February 3, 1944. However, on November 16, 1948, tragedy again stalked Ryland Milner. This time the victim was Jimmie Ryland Milner. Here is an account of what happened according to the Wednesday, November 17, 1948, *Maryville Daily Forum* which carried the headline: "Jimmie Milner Killed When Hit By Automobile":

"All Maryville was stunned today over the fatal accident last night which took the life of four-year-old Jimmie Milner, son of Mr. and Mrs. Ryland Milner . .Mr. Milner is head coach of all major sports at (Northwest) and widely known in mid-western collegiate sports circles.

The accident occurred when Jimmie and his grandmother, Mrs. E.C. Gooden, of near Ravenwood, Missouri, walked west across the street in the middle of the 100 block on North Main street at 7:20 o'clock last night (Tuesday November 16, 1948).

Before reaching the safety of the curb on the west side of the street, Mrs. Gooden and her grandson were struck by the driver of a southbound 1939 Chevrolet Coupe.

The pedestrians were in front of the Physicians Building, 116 North Main Street, when the coupe struck them.The injured boy was carried to Dr. W.R. Jackson's office in the nearby Physicians' Building.

Jimmie lived only a few minutes after reaching the Physicians' office. The 4-year-old boy suffered two basal skull fractures and a broken leg. It was learned that

Mrs. Gooden (Jimmie's grandmother) was rushed to the St. Francis hospital in an ambulance. It was reported at the hospital this morning (November 17, 1948) that the full extent of her injuries could not be determined because of the extensive shock she is suffering. It was reported, however, that she sustained a broken left shoulder, right wrist and left leg.

Mrs. Gooden and her grandson (Jimmie) were on their way to the Missouri Theater. Mr. Milner, head athletics coach at (Northwest) was attending a meeting in Stuart, Iowa, at the time of the accident."

Everett Brown, of Maryville, is a retired public relations specialist and former director of field services at Northwest. He recalls the night Jimmie died. Earlier that day, Brown said he drove Coach Milner to Stuart, Iowa, located west and north of Des Moines. He says that Coach Milner was invited to speak at a football sports ban-

Jimmie Milner

quet there. "We went to Stuart that evening," Brown recalls. "Coach Milner stood up to talk after the dinner. And then during that time the phone rang. Someone answered the phone, and called me out. Dr. W.R. Jackson in Maryville was the one that called, and Dr. Jackson was a friend of Coach Milner." Brown said he "went over to the emcee—the principal or coach—whoever was in charge of the banquet. I said 'there's been an accident with Coach Milner's son. We need to get him out of here.' So the emcee got up and stopped the banquet and told Coach Milner to come and talk to me." Brown says that Milner did not initially show any expression of amazement or anything else. He just kept saying, 'I wonder what happened?' During the drive from Stuart to Maryville, we were coming through cities, like Clarinda, Iowa, at 60 miles per hour. We were looking for someone to help us have some police escort but we didn't have anyone. We just came through. All the way home Coach Milner kept asking aloud 'How could my boy be in an accident?' That kept us busy with our thoughts all the way home—it did with me at least. Milner kept saying to me 'how bad was it?' I said, 'well Dr. Jackson said, *it's as bad as it can be.*' That was the expression he'd used. That's what I told Coach Milner. I never used the word 'killed' because I didn't know what 'as bad as it can be' meant. It could be that Jimmie was lingering some place yet in a hospital." Brown felt that if he had told Coach Milner his son was killed, "I think he would still have been wondering how did it happen. There was a car wreck or something. We didn't understand that the boy had been taken to the movie theater by his grandma and let out across the street near the theater. I guess Grandma went with him. If I would have told him Jimmie was killed, Milner would have gone very quiet and silent in the sense of shock."

By about 10:30 p.m., Brown recounts, he and Coach Milner arrived in Maryville. He escorted him to the Milner house when someone came out from the house and told Milner what had happened. Brown said he then left because Coach Milner was home and in the family's good hands. "I had done what the doctor (Jackson) had asked me to do—get him home as soon as possible. During the drive he would just sit there and stare. We'd repeat each time trying to figure why they were across the street going the other way. Brown says that over the years he found Milner to be generally as an unemotional type of fellow.

"Frankly, I thought, well, the doctor can tell him or the family can tell him his son was killed. I really didn't think it was my job or business to relay that on to him," Brown asserts.

The following is an excerpt from an article that appeared in the Thursday, November 18, 1948, front page of the *Maryville Daily Forum*: "The death of Jimmie Milner, 4-year-old son of Mr. and Mrs. Ryland Milner of Maryville was termed 'accidental without criminal negligence on the part of any one' by a coroner's jury at an inquest held Wednesday afternoon at the Price Funeral Home in Maryville."

"Nobody has gone through life without some disappointments," Milner verifies as he recalls the tragedies in his lifetime. "When you lose somebody, my wife, my first son, my twin brother it comes up when you look at some things around here in my house about my wife and my first little boy. You'll never get over those things. You moan over them I guess and talk to yourself part of the time."

Coach Milner's niece, Sue Milner McCourry, remembers Jimmie's death was devastating for both of them (Ryland and Luretta). " They were terribly terribly upset. Jimmie was a precious darling little boy. He had dark eyes and he had that pretty blond hair. Jimmie was a feisty person full of energy." Her cousin, Mary Lee Reed, adds that her uncle Ryland—after Jimmie's death—knew that if "he was going to lay down and die that was going to be the time. The whole family gathered together, and I know the family in Oklahoma City went up there to Maryville for the funeral because they weren't sure that Ryland was going to survive it." And Mrs. Reed adds, "It's really an inspirational type thing to show that uncle Ryland's spirit does live on—despite the family losses—and go on if you've got the courage to get up and walk forward." Her cousin, Sue Milner McCourry agrees and adds, "I think his competitive spirit is what has kept him here all these years. He's been out there fighting it to keep going. I hope the way uncle Ryland has coped with tragedy will be an inspiration to upcoming athletes to show what they can do."

At Jimmie's funeral, two of the pallbearers were Paul Butherus and Bill Coulter, who had played football at Maryville High School and then at Northwest. Milner also filled in as coach of the Maryville High School football team because most of the men were overseas at war. For his part, Milner was later dispatched by President Roosevelt to talk to troops overseas and let them in on news back on American soil in 1944.

Ryland Milner
Photo provided by U.S. Army Signal Corps,
Panama Canal Department

Both Butherus and Coulter have maintained regular contact with Milner, and both also live in the same town, Lexington, Missouri. Butherus was inducted in

1994 into the "M" Club Hall of Fame at Northwest. Butherus said Milner probably is able to be a survivor rather than a victim of tragic events because "he is as strong as a horse. He is always right about things. If you do this it'll make your game better. Little things you wouldn't think about and now we think of them all the time. His wife Luretta was the sweetest girl in the world and he knew it."

Adds Coulter: "Coach Milner has a gift that just demands respect. There are some people like that. I don't know if it's something he particularly did or said. It's a combination of all the things that he did and said and he expected us to respond in kind."

Coulter remembers one weekend track meet when he went out the night before with his girl-friend.

"I should have been home and in bed at least," Coulter recounts. "When I got to my car to go home, Coach Milner's car was parked right beside me and he said, 'Good evening half miler,' and I said, Coach, I'm not a half miler I'm a quarter miler and he said, *'Tomorrow you're a half miler!'*"

Coulter went on to say that he doesn't know how many athletes Milner has taught but "every one of those persons took some of Ryland Milner with them and influenced some other youngsters. Everybody that played for Ryland Milner probably felt like he was his favorite."

Coulter adds, "If Northwest had never existed, Ryland Milner would have succeeded at another university. He was that kind of man. Some university would have found him."

Howard Iba, Milner's basketball teammate at

Northwest during the 1929-1930 season, states that "every time I saw him after Jimmie's fatal accident, to me, it just seemed like that was on his mind. I wish him all the luck in the world and hope that everything keeps going good for him because Northwest officials have done a lot for Ryland and Ryland's done a lot for them up there in Maryville. That's the thing that kind of stands out for Ryland. He's had all these tragedies and he's gone along and done great—with these tragedies—which might slow a lot of people up."

Ken B. Jones, who played for Coach Milner during Jimmie's lifetime and after the boy's death adds: "As far as his professional performance, I would say he continued to coach as best he could. On a more personal basis, I'm sure, as I recall, he suffered and perhaps was not—at least for some time—quite as jovial a person. That would certainly be understandable."

Dr. Jim Redd says he's inspired by how Coach Milner responded to family tragedies. Dr. Redd lost his own wife to cancer in 1993 and credits the inspiration of Milner to cope with the loss of his beloved partner. "Well, mainly, Coach Milner had the courage to get up and keep moving every day and be around people. Loneliness can really be difficult."

Ivan Schottel of St. Joseph, says Milner has "got enough fire in him; I'll guarantee you that. After Jimmie's death he lost a lot of that fire."

On July 10, 1998, Ryland Milner received a letter from Ronald "Woodie" Wood, a former player of his who now lives in Hendersonville, Tennessee. The letter evokes the way many athletes felt about Milner particularly the fact that he was able to cope with family tragedies by maintaining a competitive spirit:

July 10, 1998

Dear Coach,

As time marches on for us both, I am more and more aware of the significance that our relationship as 'coach and basketball player' contributed to my personal life and career. The competitive spirit and desire to be a winner that you promoted as a coach has enhanced my personality for the past fifty years. As a person you were always there for encouragement and above all 'tell it like it is.' While I could never challenge you as a coach and win I still think I can win a 'one on one' with you anytime. Thanks for being a great coach and a great friend."

Respectfully yours,
Ronald "Woodie" Wood
Hendersonville, Tennessee

Long-time friend Bob Gregory emphasizes that "I know he was devastated by (family losses) but he went ahead coaching. He dealt with Jimmie's death but I know it took a lot out of him. He was able to handle this situation maybe due to some of the teaching that he had done with his players and so forth. He expected you to handle whatever you did in your athletic ability or athletic contests. If it was good, this was great. If it was bad, you had to be able to handle it. Coach Milner could of pulled into a hole and nobody would have ever been able to contact him."

Instead, Milner went from coach to director of athletics at Northwest in 1957until his retirement in 1975. Bud Tice, a former athletics trainer at Northwest, served under Milner from 1971 to 1974. He says Milner is fair and listens to what others say. "I wanted to do a lot of things different," Tice recalls. "He ran the athletic department with little or no money. He would say, 'why do you need the money now?' I've worked for a number of directors of athletics. Milner did something to me that most wouldn't do. He took me somewhat under his wing so to speak. I knew more about modern training techniques than he did, but he knew more about being an adult, being mature, being honest with people. He would not allow me ever to stray outside his guidelines. At times he would take me to his administrative office, close the door and just wonder what the heck I was doing." Tice points out that Milner became a popular administrator across the country: "This guy was respected any place he went. They knew he was an outstanding athletic director. I think his respect came because he was a good coach and he was honest and fair."

For his part, Milner said the pressure of being a coach was higher than serving as athletics director. "There were always headaches being an athletics director," he says. "I had to watch the pennies and dimes to justify what we did. Of course, we never had much money to work on. We didn't travel like they do today with all the people and things like that." Eventually, he says he grew tiresome "of all the trips you had to make and be responsible for everything. But I must say this. The players and people that I worked with in the athletic department were very cordial people."

One Northwest official in particular became a lifelong friend. Herbert Dieterich, was the long-time principal of the Horace Mann High School located on the Northwest campus. Mr. Dieterich was also Northwest's first faculty representative for the MIAA and served on the national football rules committee. Through the

In the above photo Ryland Milner (right) visits with Herbert Dieterich in a Maryville nursing home. The two friends talked every day.

years, both men uplifted each other and visited as often as they could. Milner compellingly notes, "He was a sharp old boy. We fished and hunted together. If I didn't go see him every day, I'd get a phone call from him to see how I was doing." By 1997, Dieterich was 98 years old and living in a Maryville nursing home. He died in April of that year. His son, Jack Dieterich, one of the non-military members of the undefeated 1944 V-12 football team, remembers how special Milner's visits were to the whole family during their father's last days. "Ryland's daily visit to the nursing home meant a lot to me because we always knew that Ryland was going to be there to come down and visit with Dad," Dieterich says. "He never did have a shortage of people to come visit him, but he always knew that Ryland would be there."

The younger Dieterich points out that, as long as he could remember, Milner called his father Mr. Dieterich. "He just respected Dad as being a little bit older and in an administrative position. Ryland Milner is just a remarkable person. He thinks about other people not only Dad. He's been so good to his students and the guys that played for him in football, basketball, track, golf, cross country or track and field; they always felt free to visit with him."

Adds Dieterich, "I don't think Ryland Milner's legacy can be really adequately described. He is an individual that's had so much influence over the athletic department and the young people that played for him. He's been through a lot and I think he's much like Dad. He gains a lot of support from the people that he's worked with that come back to Maryville to visit him." Ryland Milner was not the only Milner that paid respect and took time to develop a bond with Mr. Herbert Dieterich. Milner's granddaughter, Mallory, became a pen pal for Mr. Dieterich while he was in a nursing home. When he died, Mallory's mother, Sue, drove her from her home in Estherville, Iowa, to Maryville so she could attend his funeral. To be sure, the story of Ryland Milner would not be complete without visiting with his only living son, Tim Milner, his wife Sue, and their two daughters, Erin and Mallory who live in Estherville, located near the Iowa-Minnesota border.

In this April 1951 family photo Ryland Milner
holds his 16-month-old son Tim.

Chapter Eight

━━⊂⊃⊃━━

Papa Milner and
"My Little Sweethearts"

━━⊂⊃⊃━━

O N DECEMBER 20, 1949, RYLAND AND LURETTA MILNER WERE blessed with the arrival of their second son Tim. Today, Tim Milner is a successful coach and teacher in the northwest Iowa community of Estherville. He is a loving husband to his wife Sue, and he is the proud father of two girls, Erin and Mallory, or as Ryland Milner calls his granddaughters, "My little sweethearts."

Tim also speaks proudly of his father. "He (Ryland Milner) was very, very easy to grow up under. I can only remember him really disciplining me once. I didn't cause too many problems. I just remember one time and that was when I laughed at my Mom when she broke a yardstick over me and it didn't hurt." Milner explains how it all happened: "Mom made the comment she hated sparrows in her bird feeder. So the good kid I am I get a BB gun for Christmas. So I'm sitting in the kitchen sink shooting out of the open kitchen window— shooting only the sparrows, mind you, off the bird feeder. She came home from where ever she was and there were about fifteen to twenty dead sparrows laying down there. She got a yardstick after me, and it broke on the first swing and I kind of laughed at her. Then Dad got home. I think I might have hit every wall in the house once." However, Tim says his father, while only five-foot eight inches tall, commanded respect: "I don't think it was anything he ever said or did. All he had to do is look at you. I can remember the stare."

Tim Milner says his parents told him about his brother Jimmie. "Oh, I suppose it was probably the age of ten or eleven or twelve where I could really realize it." He credits his parents for being sensitive to his needs as they told him that his older brother was killed. "I guess it was a subject that was never brought up much around home," Tim says. "To me maybe the only reason I'm here is because that (Jimmie's fatal accident) happened. I don't know. That happened in November (1948) and I was born the next December (1949)." Tim Milner does remember that religion, after Jimmie died, "kind of dropped out of our family for awhile."

He describes his mother, Luretta, this way: "She might have been five foot one, and got up all the way to 120 pounds when she was pregnant with me, but generally she was about five feet one and 95 or 100 pounds. She was a very little woman. Very hard working. She never really worked out of the home. She did a lot of yard work. She also tended to a garden. She was just kind of a bubbly fun-loving person. She was outgoing. She liked people around to socialize. But, she was a homebody too. My mother was a person that was always there for you. Very kind. Would do anything for anybody that she possibly could. Dad is essentially the same way. They were, I would say, very much in love. They were very supportive of each other. They were there for each other all the time. They virtually didn't do something without the other unless it was school-related business. Mom went to everything (athletic events) she could while Dad was coaching and supported him in every way." Tim feels the best advice his Mom and Dad gave him was "just be yourself and treat people the way you want to be treated."

Tim comments that he was never forced to participate in athletics by either parent. "Well, it was important to me because I loved athletics. I was brought up around it, and I wanted to be the best that I could be and I was supported every way possible. I'm sure I was led towards athletics being the son of a football coach. When I was little, he was still a football coach at Northwest and I went to school right there on campus (Horace Mann school) through the eighth grade. Until eighth grade, I'd go down to his office after school and sit around or go out in the gym and shoot baskets. So I was around athletics. There wasn't any question in my mind that I wanted to be an athlete."

Tim Milner is adamant about which sports he enjoyed while growing up. "My favorite sport from the time I was knee high was baseball and then golf and basketball and probably football was my fourth favorite. I participated in all four of them at Maryville High School. I had the ability to pitch and throw hard for my age, and I was always competing against older kids because I was the youngest in my class." Interestingly, his favorite sport, baseball, was not offered during the whole time he was in high school. Instead, Tim played Legion ball against area teams. "I played as a seventh-grader legion pitcher and then I played about every position. I threw 94 miles per hour."

Tim Milner recalls the days when he was participating in high school sports while his father was athletics director at Northwest and also served as a football and basketball referee. "He came to see me play when he wasn't refereeing. He was pretty busy with college athletics but he was there whenever he could be." Milner explained that athletics took up his whole time and he did not have time to participate in other school activity programs. "My parents wanted me to participate but yet there was never any forcing if I didn't want to do something," Tim recounts. "Theone thing my parents always said was if you start something, you're going to finish it and that's kind of the way my wife Sue and I have raised our two daughters, Erin and Mallory."

Tim Milner went on to say that he is not jealous that athletes through the years have referred to Coach Ryland Milner as a father figure. "I think it's a great tribute to him," Tim said. " My mom was a mother figure to all of them too. I can remember several times people not having a place to eat, and Dad would bring them home and Mom would throw in extra noodles or dumplings or something we were having. We made do. Dad never went after glory, never sought glory and I think that's the way I was raised."

Tim Milner earned a Bachelor of Science degree in health and physical education in secondary education from Northwest in 1971. After graduation, his lifelong dream to be a professional baseball player began to materialize. "That was the number one thing in my mind. If I didn't make it as a professional baseball player, I wanted to be a baseball coach and a football coach. I played, of course, at Northwest four years, and then in the summers I was playing at Clarinda, Iowa, for the Athletics. From there I went on to Central Michigan graduate school and received my Master's Degree in 1972 in health education. I came back in the summer of 1972 and played baseball at Clarinda."

Eventually, Tim went to Jacksonville, Florida, and taught school for a year. He mentions that "in Jacksonville, I was playing on like a city league, or semi-pro league. I happened to be seen and was offered a free-agent contract with the New York Mets in 1973. I was in their farm system for three years. I went to spring training my last year as a non-roster player, and I did pitch in one spring training game," Tim says. " He then went back into the minor leagues and started in AAA and went to AA and finally ended up as a player coach in A ball. "That's when I kind of hurt my shoulder and decided it was time to get out and go on. At that time the rotator cuff surgery was just starting and they weren't very successful with it." During the 1975-1976 school year, Tim worked as an admissions recruiter for Northwest His coverage area was the state of Iowa.

"Then I took a job in Estherville as the baseball coach and physical education teacher. Now I'm fifth through eighth grade P.E. teacher, assistant football coach and head golf coach. I coached baseball and was head girls' golf coach," Tim notes. He also points out that his parents taught him how to play golf when he was five or six years old.

Tim says education was very important while growing up under his parents. "I was never grounded because I made poor grades or anything like that. All the years I think I probably had one D which never made them happy. Good grades were expected of me. That D grade was in college in political science, and I was just happy to get out of there with a D."

Tim Milner remembers when his Mom began to get sick during the late 1970s. "She had never really been sick a day in her life until about the last three or four years. She had a bad case of the flu, and I don't think she ever really recovered from it. At the time, my father was the only one that had ever been sick, serious. He had a heart attack and had open heart surgery and all of that and truthfully probably wasn't expected to live very much longer. And here's my Mom—had never been sick—and then when I saw how sick she actually was, she could have been kept alive by just laying there. No I didn't want that. (On March 9, 1980) when her time came and I saw her suffering in the hospital struggling to breathe and that type of thing, I said 'it's time to let go' and she passed away. It was very tough on my father. They were very much in love. Nearly forty-six years they were married. I never heard them argue once—never heard them yell once. I guess I try to pattern myself after that with my wife, Sue, and our two daughters."

Ryland Milner lovingly calls his two granddaughters "My little sweethearts." Erin was born May 17, 1983, and Mallory was born on February 5, 1987. They, in turn, love talking about their grandfather, lovingly known as their Papa Milner. "I don't know. Papa Milner's just a neat guy. He's fun when we go down there to Maryville. We go to the gym and we do fun stuff together," Erin says. Meanwhile, Mallory adds: "And every time we go to Northwest he goes 'do you know your name's on that complex?'" Indeed, among the men and women listed on the Ryland Milner Complex wall plaque are the names of both his granddaughters. Erin said she is always impressed that he walks virtually every day down the hallways at Northwest's athletics office: "I mean people are going to see him and

Pictured above (left to right) are Mallory, Sue, Tim, Ryland and Erin.

talk to him and stuff. Every time we go he introduces us to them," Mallory agrees with her older sister. "You can't go anywhere in Maryville and meet somebody that doesn't know Papa Milner." The two girls say they talk to their Papa Milner usually every Sunday night. "If my Dad doesn't call him," Erin said, "Papa Milner will call us." Each granddaughter talks about 10 minutes with their grandfather.

Erin relates that with the many honors bestowed upon Papa Milner she likes the fact that he is "a good guy." "Yea," Mallory says. "He's like known everywhere in Maryville." Erin says Papa Milner always encour-

ages them. Mallory says her Papa Milner "just wants
you to do the best that you can do." Erin thinks her grandfather has so much energy, while her sister Mallory points
out her Papa Milner "helps people go their own ways
and he won't take the credit all for himself."

Ryland Milner's two little sweethearts will always
remember the advice given by their Papa Milner: "Never
say you can't," Erin recalls. "Always try," adds Mallory
whose middle name is Luretta just like her
grandmother's.

In the photo above are (left to right) Erin, Papa Milner and Mallory.

During the summer of 1998, Ryland Milner sometimes stayed with Tim Milner and his family at their
cabin which offers a breathtaking view of the North
Spirit Lake area in northern Iowa. With the cool breeze
of the lakefront and drinking glasses of cold water, I
joined the two men on the deck to soak up the good
weather. I ask Ryland Milner to tell me about his son.

His reply tells me: "None any better than Tim. He was all we had. Nothing in the world is ahead of him as far as I'm concerned. Tim graciously interrupts and says "yea, there is. . .two granddaughters. Tim looks at his Dad and turns to me to say,"What I've learned from Dad is that if you're well respected great things can happen for you. Dad has never asked for the limelight. He just says to always do what's right."

Ryland Milner listens to his son and tells him: "Just being on the earth with me is enough, Tim"

The conversation next turned to the tragic losses during Milner's lifetime. The elder Milner turns towards his son and says, "You know Tim, talking about the loss of loved ones including your brother, Jimmie and your Mom, Luretta—take them to bed with you but shake them off during the night." Tears began to well in his eyes behind his eyeglasses. He looks at his son and adds, "One of the most special memories of you my son was the day you were born. I thank the Lord for a young man." A son born to a dear coach.

And so, as Ryland Milner continues to pace the halls back at Northwest, the well-known and well-liked coach shares two special letters. The first letter went like this:

October 25, 1957

Dear Coach:

I am very sorry I cannot come back for Homecoming this year for I would like to be there for the game and especially for the half-time ceremonies honoring Ryland Milner.

I had the pleasure of coaching (you) in high school and also in college at Northwest Missouri Teachers College. In my coaching experience I have never met a finer

young man or a more efficient coach...(You) have done
an exceptionally fine job for the college down through
the years and (your) influence and associations with the
young men who have been out for athletics at the college
is appreciated by all.

Sincerely,
Henry P. Iba
Director of Athletics
Oklahoma State University
Stillwater, Oklahoma

As Coach Milner remembers that letter, he shows
me the Irish crystal basketball, an award named in Mr.
Iba's honor. Milner then glances at the nearby Irish
crystal football named in his honor. All he can do is
smile and keep walking. We ride back up the elevator
to the second floor. This time, when he stops to look at
the plaque with the names of the Ryland Milner Scholarship, he remembers a 1998 letter from one of his
former players, George Nathan who helped launch the
scholarship fund drive and graduated from Northwest
in 1954. Nathan now lives in California:

Dear Coach:
The Ryland Milner scholarship fund came about
because of a genuine love for you by many of your former
players. Your toughness and tenderness toward all your
former students and players is legendary. We now honor
you with this scholarship in your name. We accom-
plished what we set out to do and you are still Mr.
Bearcat to the many thousands of students you coached
and taught over the sixty years of your life.
Personally, your help in my graduating in 1954 was
a very positive influence on my life. Trust that all those

whose lives you had something to do with share the same
thoughts of our dear coach."

>   Sincerely,
>   George Nathan
>   Class of 1954

As I watch Coach Milner walk down the hall, I think what a wonderful life he has had—and still has. During the approximately one year I spent in the life of this man, I was amazed at how many people truly love and respect him. The love was returned to this well-known coach during a 79th birthday surprise at the 1988 homecoming football game. School officials presented the retired former Bearcat athlete, coach and athletics director with a giant 10-foot-long, three-foot wide birthday cake in the shape of a football field, complete with figurines of players and both goal posts. The

During the 1988 Homecoming game, Northwest officials presented the retired Ryland Milner a giant birthday cake shaped like a football field. The cake was shared with university alumni, faculty and staff.

Bearcat Marching Band did a rendition of "Happy Birthday" and the crowd joined in. Later the cake was shared with alumni, and university faculty and staff who came out of the crowd to help Milner celebrate his birthday.

After spending countless hours with him, I am reminded of the words from my beloved mother, Priscilla S. Mares, who died in 1995: "Help me to fulfill the purpose for which I have been created and share my abilities—not only to help myself—but to help others." Her words came to life the more I delved into Coach Milner's life. He certainly has fulfilled his purpose and consistently shared his abilities with others. Indeed, he has inspired me to believe that the quality of life is more important than the quantity of awards, tributes and so forth. Ryland Milner *lives for today*. His amazing zest for life is contagious. He wants to meet new people at Northwest. Asked why he takes the time to visit with students, he replies, "I stay near young people because they keep me young." About this time, a couple of students come down the hallway. He introduces himself. "Hi, they call me Coach Milner. Have you got time for a little story?..."

Chapter Nine

—◦◻◦—

Coach Milner: His View

—◦◻◦—

I thank the Lord every morning not at night but in the morning when I get up. It wouldn't hurt to do it both times.

—◦◻◦—

I've enjoyed life, I mean, of course ups and downs have derailed me to a certain degree but the people have been awful good to me.

—◦◻◦—

Many nights when I was coaching I would lie there in bed and I couldn't even close my eyes thinking of what I should do tomorrow in certain conditions, especially if the weather was bad or something like that. . .I got pretty rowdy at night before a ball game.

—◦◻◦—

When asked if he viewed life as a glass of water half full or half empty, he replies: I just drink it. I'm probably optimistic most of the time to a certain degree I guess.

—◦◻◦—

No, I didn't go out there to please people. I went out there to do a job that would be valuable to the public, the boys and everything else.

It didn't matter if I was criticized by others. Sometimes it'd stir you up a little bit so you try harder. If you're not waiting for something like that—you're not a coach.

If you're living in the past, pretty soon you're just going to be up here and everybody else has left you; they've gone by.

There's nobody living today that hasn't had a failure or something whether he was a little kid or grown up. Well, how many things have you said or I've said ' I can't do it.' You know if you put out a little extra energy you could do it.

Never forget the word respect. If I don't have respect for people, how can I expect them to have respect for me?

If you don't have something up there you're working towards, you're never going to get there.

I didn't want to lose. I'd lose but I didn't want to.

Right now there's an object up there that you want to get to. If you don't want to be the best —don't go. What I mean by that now you're working up if you get to a certain point and you just halfway quit in your own self you're not treating yourself right.

My theory is to be able to improve in everyday life. I want to be there. I want to get here. I felt like that all my life. That's what you always tell the athletes—do the best you can.

If you don't work as hard as you can work and do the job as you think it should be, you're in trouble.

I don't know just why we go some place instead of the others. Somebody had to be there that you had confidence and faith in that was going to change your directions.

I'm not scared of death. I think when the Good Lord wants me He's going to take me—that's between the two of us!

I had kids they didn't know anything about athletics or anything but they had a will. If there's a will there's a way.

There wouldn't be any such thing as athletics today if you didn't care whether you won or lost. You got to do your best. Emphasize best if you want to progress.

I kind of lived on the theory to do it my way and if it's wrong I'll take the blame for it.

That is a nasty word—perfectionist. It's something you have to build up to. If you don't try to improve and get out there, you're just going to go down hill.

———

I've always felt when you lose a ball game you lose it on mistakes. That's the thing that always bothered me more than anything else.

———

Character is respect for other people. Character is never changed as far as I'm concerned. Win if you can with character.

———

The only trouble I ever had with somebody is if somebody comes up and criticizes one of my boys. We might have a fight. I have faith in my players. I love them.

———

A coach can't do it by himself or herself. The whole group, you got to get the whole group ready at one time. Get them ready. Togetherness is the most important thing. Pulling for one another every way you go.

———

When you're wrong do you admit it? Why, heck, yes I admit it. You're not still alive if you haven't been wrong. Your athletes have got to have faith in you.

———

My whole theory for all of the athletes is you're here to play a sport, but, first of all, you're here to get a degree. Your grades do down, you go down.

I don't think there's anything that hurts a young buck any worse than a coach sitting over there putting him in the ball game, and maybe he makes a mistake or something or run one play or two and jerk him right out. What are we teaching?

⸺◦⊂⊃◦⸺

If the report comes back to me that he's failing real low and he's been notified of it, and another report comes, I don't give a darn if he's President of the United States. He's not going to play.

⸺◦⊂⊃◦⸺

I haven't seen anybody, hardly in my day, that was so out of line that I couldn't straighten up.

⸺◦⊂⊃◦⸺

Pointing to his head: you've got to have it up here. Pointing to his heart: first of all right here. All kids are not the same.

⸺◦⊂⊃◦⸺

Winning coaches are the ones that suffer more than the mediocre ones coaching. The pressure's up here so much from the outsiders and the people in the stands.

⸺◦⊂⊃◦⸺

I never can ever remember anybody bigger than me. In athletics and you're the coach nobody is bigger than you. Size yes. But up here (pointing to his head) no.

⸺◦⊂⊃◦⸺

One thing I didn't tolerate in my coaching was talking back to me.

Be available as much as anything else. I mean I felt I've always been available to help anybody to do something.

———◈———

Define success: Doing the best you can do in all situations if it's a win. I don't like to lose; don't get me wrong. I don't like to lose.

———◈———

On listening to games on the radio: the other day I got more worked up sitting here than I did when I was coaching out there. Well, you've been at it so long you got it in your system, and there's not a way to get it out. I have to blow it out. I get up and walk around in circles.

———◈———

The idea of winning at all costs when it gets to that point, and pressure is so built up on these youngsters that's not right. Had to win? It was never brought up to us like that.

———◈———

Respect. I'll tell you one thing now and you write that down and rewrite it and write it and write it. The quote that Coach Henry Iba made to us in a group at Classen High School in Oklahoma City. Although he was probably five years older than most of us, he said, *'I don't give a darn whether you like me or not. All I ask is respect.'* That quote is universal.

On December 16, 1988, Ryland Milner was inducted into the Missouri Sports Hall of Fame. He received his award from his mentor the late Henry Iba shown on the right.

Chronology

1859: July 3 – John Jonathan Milner, father of Ryland Milner, born.

1872: October 4 – Drucilla Olivia Pope, mother of Ryland Milner, born.

1905: August 4 – Missouri Governor Joseph W. Folk approved and notified Maryville residents that Maryville had been selected as the site of the Normal School for Northwest Missouri.

1906: January 4 – Mr. Frank Deerwester selected as first president of normal school.
June 13 – First session of the Fifth District Normal School opened; training school also opened.

1907: May 27 – Mr. Homer Martien Cook named as president.
July 15 – First athletics director, Paul A. White, employed.
September 16 – Men of the Normal School organized for football practice.

1909: July 19 – Dr. H.K. Taylor elected president.
September 20 – Emmett Scott employed to coach football.
September 24 – Ryland Harp Milner and Jimmie Brown Milner were born in Glen Cove, Texas.

1912: November 1 – Luretta Gooden born at Parnell, Missouri.

1913: May 19 – Resignation of Dr. H.K. Taylor, president, accepted; Mr. Ira Richardson, head of Education department, elected president.

1921: June 6 – Mr. Uel W. Lamkin was elected president to succeed President Richardson.

1926: October 18 – Billy Lamkin, son of President and Mrs. Lamkin, died.

1929: May 29 – Ryland Milner graduates from Classen High School in Oklahoma City.
Fall – Ryland Milner enrolls at Maryville State Teachers College.

1929: September 1 – Mr. Henry Iba came to assist E.A. "Lefty" Davis in the Physical Education department at Maryville State Teachers College.

1930: July 8 – Death of Dickie Lamkin (Clement Dickinson Lamkin) son of President and Mrs. Lamkin.

1933: March 20 – Ryland Milner's father, John Jonathan, dies.
Spring – Ryland Milner graduates from the Maryville State Teachers College and is hired to coach football at Jackson High School in southeast Missouri.

October 3 – Wilbur "Sparky" Stalcup named to the faculty in physical education at Maryville State Teachers College.

1934: December 26 – Ryland Milner marries Luretta Gooden.

1937: May 25 – Ryland Milner employed in the physical education department at the Maryville State Teacher's College.

1943: July 1 – Four hundred Navy men enrolled in the College for the V-12 program.

1944: February 3 – James "Jimmie" Ryland Milner born to Luretta and Ryland Milner in Maryville.

1945: March 6 – Coach Ryland Milner left for overseas to help in an athletic clinic for army officers who would coach service men.
September 17 – The Board of Regents accepted the resignation of President Lamkin and named Dr. J.W. Jones to succeed him.
December 18 – Coach Wilbur "Sparky" Stalcup, on terminal leave from the Navy, resumed his work as coach and director of personnel for men.

1948: November 16 – Jimmie Milner, son of Ryland and Luretta Milner, killed in a traffic accident in downtown Maryville.

1949: December 20 – Tim Milner is born to Ryland and Luretta Milner in Maryville.

1959: May 18 – Ryland Milner's mother, Drucilla Olivia Milner, dies.

1978: Distinguished Alumni Award presented to Mr. Henry Iba, member of the class of 1928.

1980: March 9 – Luretta Milner dies.
Fall – Henry Iba inducted into the M Club Hall of Fame.

1981: Fall – Ryland Milner inducted into the M Club Hall of Fame.

1983: May 17 – Granddaughter Erin Milner is born.

1987: February 5 – A second granddaughter, Mallory, is born.
October 9 – Coach Ryland Milner receives the Distinguished Alumni Award presented by Northwest.
October 10 – The University officially honors Ryland Milner by naming the athletics facilities as simply the Ryland Milner Complex.

1988: December 16 – Coach Ryland Milner inducted into the Missouri Sports Hall of Fame.

1994: October 14 – Coach Ryland Milner receives plaque in recognition of dedication and Commitment to Northwest Missouri State University and the U.S. Navy V-12 Personnel of World War II.

Honors

Northwest Missouri State University Athletic Hall of Fame Induction 1981

———◦⊂▭⊃◦———

Athlete and Coach
Ryland "Taffy" Milner
Sept. 24, 1909 -

ATHLETE: 1929-33

Oklahoma State H.S. Basketball Champs - 1929

All State and All American: 1929

Okla. State H.S. Baseball Champs: 1927-29

All State: 1927-29

Outstanding Athlete: Classen H.S. - 1929

M.I.A.A. Championship Football Team - 1931
   Undefeated in football 1931 (9-0)

M.I.A.A. Championship Basketball Team:
   1929-30, 1931-32, 1932-33
   Undefeated in 1929-30 (31-0)
   M.I.A.A. All Conference:1932-33

COACH: 1934-75

Jackson High School (1934-37)

Football - undefeated- unscored upon 1935
Four year record (32-3-0)

Basketball - State champions: 1933-1934
Four-year record (70-12)

Track - Head Coach- four years

Northwest (1937-1975)

Football: 1937-57 (1945 no football)
M.I.A.A. Champions or Co-Champions
1938, 1939, 1941, 1942, 1948, 1952
Twenty Year Period (90-63-13)

Basketball: 1943-50
Seven Year Record (70-59)

Track: 1946-50
M.I.A.A. Champions Indoor: 1949, 1950
M.I.A.A. Champions Outdoor: 1949, 1950

Golf: 1947-75

Cross Country: 1958-62

Index